CW00344342

SYDNEY
ENCOUNTER

CHARLES RAWLINGS-WAY

Sydney Encounter
Published by Lonely Planet Publications Pty Ltd
ABN 36 005 607 983

Australia	Head Office, Locked Bag 1, Footscray, Vic 3011
	☎ 03 8379 8000 fax 03 8379 8111
	talk2us@lonelyplanet.com.au
USA	150 Linden St, Oakland, CA 94607
	☎ 510 250 6400
	toll free 800 275 8555
	fax 510 893 8572
	info@lonelyplanet.com
UK	2nd fl, 186 City Rd, London EC1V 2NT
	☎ 020 7106 2100 fax 020 7106 2101
	go@lonelyplanet.co.uk

This guidebook was commissioned in Lonely Planet's Melbourne office, and produced by the following: **Commissioning Editors** Emma Gilmour, Maryanne Netto **Coordinating Editor** Shawn Low **Coordinating Cartographer** Valeska Cañas **Coordinating Layout Designer** Paul Iacono **Assisting Editor** Kate Evans **Assisting Cartographer** Enes Basic **Managing Editor** Annelies Mertens **Managing Cartographer** Alison Lyall **Cover** Image research provided by lonelyplanetimages. com **Project Manager** Chris Girdler **Thanks to** Jessica Boland, David Connolly, Sally Darmody, Laura Jane

Our Readers Many thanks to the travellers who wrote to us with helpful hints, useful advice and interesting anecdotes: Coral Anderson, Maureen Ball, Richard Beatty, Nigel Chent, Sue Davidson, Elaine Evans, Richard Francis, Alexia Hollands, Anthony Keogh, Silke Kerwick, Rebecca Larratt, Julie Macklin, Norm & Mary Mainland, Alan Morrison, Lindsay Petrie, Peter Saundry, Ken Sutherland.

ISBN 978 1 74104 920 6

10 9 8 7 6 5 4 3

Printed by Hang Tai Printing Company, Hong Kong.
Printed in China.

Acknowledgements Sydney Ferries Network Map © Sydney Ferries 2008; Sydney City Rail Map © RailCorp 2009

MIX
Paper from responsible sources
FSC
www.fsc.org
FSC™ C021741

HOW TO USE THIS BOOK
Colour-Coding & Maps
Colour-coding is used for symbols on maps and in the text that they relate to (eg all eating venues on the maps and in the text are given a green fork symbol). Each neighbourhood also gets its own colour, and this is used down the edge of the page and throughout that neighbourhood section.

Shaded yellow areas on the maps denote 'areas of interest' – for their historical significance, their attractive architecture or their great bars and restaurants. We encourage you to head to these areas and just start exploring!

Prices
Multiple prices listed with reviews (eg $10/5 or $10/5/20) indicate adult/child, adult/concession or adult/child/family.

CHARLES RAWLINGS-WAY

Born in Devonshire and transported to Tasmania when he was three, Charles lusted after Sydney for far too long before mustering the nerve to ask for a date. And to his amazement, she said yes! The city's cool bars and warm beaches proved predictably seductive – lust soon turned into love and an inescapable fascination.

A lapsed architect, underrated rock guitarist, optimistic home renovator and confirmed hedonist, Charles greased the production cogs at Lonely Planet's Melbourne HQ for many moons before hitting the open road as a freelance travel writer a few years ago. Now an Adelaidean, he regularly flees SA for a walk on Sydney's wild side, and to visit his mum.

CHARLES' THANKS

Thanks to the following for their input, generosity and friendship during the creation of this book: Maryanne Netto, Tashi Wheeler and Errol Hunt, Mona and Olivia Rawlings-Way, Warren and Nathan Jones, Jay Chinchen, Rodney and Sandra Renshaw, Gerard Reinmuth, Andrew P Street, Sophie Du Bois, Ristin Nichols and Ted Vanderhoek, Gaetano Palmese and the LP production crew.

Above all, thank you Meg and Ione for our truly inescapable fascination.

THE PHOTOGRAPHER

With a burning desire to document the unusual, Travis Drever has spent a good part of the last two decades snapping happily at anything that takes his fancy. Shooting for a varied range of corporates including *The Herald and Weekly Times* and *mX* as well as donating his services to *MiniBar Magazine* and *The Green Left Weekly,* he now has a Lonely Planet commission under his belt. Australian-born, Travis has had to clock up many a frequent flyer-point in his plight to find that perfect image: he has travelled throughout Asia and lived in Spain, Sweden, Holland, England and France.

Cover photograph A perfect summer afternoon at Bondi Beach, Mike V/Photolibrary. **Internal photographs** p82 by Charles Rawlings-Way; p93 Daniel Boud/Time Out Sydney; p18 Jenni Carter/Art Gallery of New South Wales; p20 courtesy the City of Sydney; p101, p135, p137 Peter Dragicevich; p130 Marie-Louise Holst; p21 courtesy Tropfest; p159 Ben Symons/courtesy the artist and Annandale Galleries, Sydney. All other photographs by Lonely Planet Images, and by Travis Drever except p4, p6 Oliver Strewe; p12 Claver Carroll; p19 John Borthwick; p22, p40 Paul Beinssen; p34 Glenn Beanland; p46, p70, p115, p149, p151 Greg Elms; p58 Dennis Jones.

All images are copyright of the photographers unless otherwise indicated. Many of the images in this guide are available for licensing from **Lonely Planet Images:** www.lonelyplanetimages.com

CONTENTS

THIS IS SYDNEY

At the heart of Sydney – Australia's oldest, largest and most diverse city – is the outrageously good-looking Sydney Harbour. Like a psychedelic supermodel, the city curves and sways through a glamorous maze of sandstone headlands, lazy bays and legendary surf beaches.

The Sydney experience is essentially physical: dunk yourself in the Bondi surf, sail under the Harbour Bridge on a yacht, jog along the Bondi clifftops or just yell yourself hoarse at a rugby match. Outside is where you want to be – the beaches swarm, street cafés buzz and the harbour blooms with sails.

No less culturally complex than it is on the map, Sydney is the landing point for most of Australia's immigrants. An edgy multiculturalism ignites the city's food scene and fuels its nocturnal life – you'll lose yourself in the restaurants, bars and dance clubs just as easily as on the streets. Aboriginal heritage makes an impact through art – a crop of excellent urban galleries celebrating indigenous culture.

Jealous as hell, the rest of Australia stereotypes Sydney as more body-beautiful than bookish, more *carpe diem* than museum – a narcissistic 'Sin City' fixated on sunglasses, salons and soy lattes. Sure, there's a lot of blonde dye in Bondi, but Sydney's citizens are no prettier than anyone else. The genetic legacy of the British and Irish convicts who built the city is more evident in the city's dogged self-belief than anything mirror-worthy. Make no mistake – Sydneysiders invest heavily in aesthetics, but their infectious, gutsy energy overrides the glam and relegates big-city cynicism, suburban sprawl and occasional racial friction to the back of their collective mind.

From squalid and desperate penal beginnings, it's no small irony that Sydney has evolved into a sparkling, progressive metropolis defined by optimism and staggering natural beauty. The rest of Australia is in denial – Sydney is as good as it gets!

Top Left Opera Bar (p59) Top Right Boathouse on Blackwattle Bay (p81) Bottom Bronte Beach (p14)

>HIGHLIGHTS

Browse for classy souvenirs in the Opera House Shop

>1 SYDNEY OPERA HOUSE

SWOON BENEATH THE HEAVEN-SENT CURVES OF THE SYDNEY OPERA HOUSE

Aghast with admiration for the Sydney Opera House, famous architect Louis Kahn said: 'The sun did not know how beautiful its light was until it was reflected off this building.' Danish architect Jørn Utzon's competition-winning 1956 design is Australia's most recognisable icon. Utzon is rumoured to have drawn inspiration from orange segments, palm fronds and Mayan temples, and the building has been poetically likened to a typewriter stuffed with scallop shells and the sexual congress of turtles. Viewed from any angle it's architecturally orgasmic, but the ferry view approaching Circular Quay is hard to beat.

The predicted four-year construction started in 1959. After a tumultuous tirade of ego clashes, delays, politicking, death and cost blowouts, Utzon quit in disgust in 1966. The Opera House finally opened in 1973. Unembittered, Utzon and his son Jan were commissioned for renovations in 2004. Utzon died in 2008.

Inside are six venues where dance, concerts, opera and theatre are staged (p62), plus the left-of-centre studio for emerging artists. The acoustics are superb; the internal aesthetics like the belly of a whale. Most events (2400 of them annually!) sell out quickly, but partial-view tickets are often available on short notice. There's also an artsy Sunday market on the concourse (p54).

See also p53.

>2 SYDNEY HARBOUR BRIDGE

TRAVEL ACROSS, OVER OR UNDER THE SYDNEY HARBOUR BRIDGE

Whether they're driving over it, climbing up it, rollerblading across it or sailing under it, Sydneysiders adore their bridge and swarm around it like ants on ice cream. Dubbed the 'old coat hanger', it's a spookily big object – moving around town you'll catch sight of it out of the corner of your eye and get a fright! Perhaps Sydney poet Kenneth Slessor said it best: 'Day and night, the bridge trembles and echoes like a living thing.'

The bridge links the central business district (CBD) with North Sydney, crossing the harbour at one of its narrowest points. The two halves of chief engineer JJC Bradfield's mighty arch – 134m high and 502m long – were built outwards from each shore. In 1932, after nine years of merciless toil, the two arches were only centimetres apart when 100km/h winds set them swaying. The coat hanger hung tough and the arch was soon completed. In 2007 the bridge turned 75.

The best way to experience the bridge is on foot – don't expect much of a view crossing by car or train. Staircases access the bridge from both shores; a footpath runs along its eastern side. If this view doesn't sate you, try a knee-trembling BridgeClimb (p60) or scale the southeast pylon to the Pylon Lookout Museum.

See also p52.

>3 SYDNEY HARBOUR

SAIL OUT ONTO SYDNEY HARBOUR, THE WET ESSENCE OF SYDNEY

When convicted murderer Francis Morgan stood on the Pinchgut Island gallows in 1797, about to hang, he gazed wistfully across Sydney Harbour and uttered, 'Well, you have here indeed a most beautiful harbour.' Morgan had a point. Stretching 20km inland, the harbour is the shimmering soul of Sydney, its beaches, coves, bays, islands and waterside parks providing crucial relief from the ordeals of urban life. Crisscrossed by ferries and carpeted by yachts, it's both the city's playground and a major port.

The chardonnay way to experience Sydney Harbour is to go sailing (p75). Alternatively, catch the ferry to Manly (p132), swim at Shark Bay (p15), dine with harbour views at Circular Quay (p55), or chase the harbour upstream to Parramatta (p27) on a RiverCat (p175).

Sydney Harbour National Park protects pockets of harbourside bushland (with some magical walking tracks including the Manly Scenic Walkway, p142) and five harbour islands. Clark, Shark and Rodd islands are chilled-out picnic spots – the Sydney Visitor Centre (p180) provides access info. Goat Island and Fort Denison (aka 'Pinchgut') were once hellish convict gulags. Goat Island is off-limits, but the National Parks & Wildlife Service (p180) runs Fort Denison tours.

North Head and South Head form the gateway to the harbour. Our South Head Shuffle walking tour (p143) takes in Watsons Bay and The Gap, an epic clifftop lookout.

>4 KINGS CROSS & AROUND

SLICE THROUGH THE VICE AROUND KINGS CROSS, SYDNEY'S EDGIEST ENCLAVE

Riding high above the CBD beneath the big Coca-Cola sign (as much a Sydney icon as LA's Hollywood sign), 'the Cross' is a bizarre, densely populated dichotomy of good and evil. Strip joints, tacky tourist shops and backpacker hostels bang heads with classy restaurants, funky bars and gorgeous guesthouses as the Cross pumps 24/7. A weird cross-section of society is drawn to the lights – buskers, beggars, tourists, prostitutes, pimps, groomed metrosexuals, horny businessmen and underfed artists roam the streets on equal footing. The Cross rocks.

Smitten with a hooker in his ode 'Darling It Hurts', brilliant Aussie songwriter Paul Kelly sang, 'Darling it hurts to see you down in Darlinghurst tonight'. Kings Cross prostitutes rarely venture across William St into Darlinghurst these days – there are too many cinematographers and caffeinated students wanting to smell the action without necessarily getting involved.

Woolloomooloo, down McElhone Stairs from the Cross, has also cleaned up its act. Harry's Café de Wheels (p103) and the sailors remain, but things are begrudgingly less pugilistic than in the past.

Gracious, tree-lined Potts Point and Elizabeth Bay seem worlds away. Well-preserved Victorian, Edwardian and Art Deco houses and flats flank picturesque avenues. Elizabeth Bay House (p97) is a must-see.

See also p96.

HIGHLIGHTS

>5 BEACHES, BEACHES, BEACHES

CARVE UP THE SURF OR SUN YOURSELF SILLY ON SYDNEY'S FABULOUS BEACHES

Sydney's beaches – protected harbour enclaves and surf-pummelled ocean shores – teem with weekend life, but Sydneysiders also swim before, after or instead of going to work. Most beaches are clean, accessible and patrolled by surf lifesavers. Many beaches are topless; a couple are nude (when in Rome…).

Definitively Sydney, Bondi is one of the world's great beaches – the Pacific arrives in great foaming swells and all people are equal, as democratic as sand. It's the closest ocean beach to the city, has good waves and is great for a rough 'n' tumble swim. Don't miss the Bondi Pavilion (p123), Sunday's Bondi Markets (p123), the Bondi-to-Bronte Clifftop Trail (p140) and the Eora Aboriginal rock engravings near the cliffs at the Bondi Golf Club, north of the beach.

South of Bondi are Tamarama, Bronte, Coogee, Maroubra and Cronulla beaches. Fully deserving of the nickname 'Glamarama', Tamarama's deep, sexy gulch attracts the generically gorgeous. Bronte is a small family-oriented beach with a perfect rock pool and a string of beachy cafés. Coogee is an Aboriginal word for rotting seaweed, but don't let that deter you – the beach is wide and handsome. Maroubra rivals Bondi for size and swell, but it's far more relaxed. Cronulla's *looong* surf beach stretches towards Botany Bay's refineries. It's an edgy place, the ragged sense of impending 'something' erupting into racial violence in late 2005.

Worthy harbour beaches include Camp Cove, Shark Bay and Balmoral. Camp Cove is a gorgeous golden beach frequented by Watsons Bay families and topless beach babes. Despite the name, there's really nothing to worry about at Shark Bay – a hefty net protects swimmers from becoming something's lunch. Balmoral is popular with picnicking North Shore families, swimmers, kayakers and windsurfers.

Beyond Manly, King of the Northern Beaches, are dozens of beaut beaches. Capped by Barrenjoey Lighthouse, Palm Beach is a meniscus of bliss. Nudists nude-up to the north, million-dollar real estate booms in the south and cheesy TV soap *Home & Away* is filmed somewhere in between. Sleepy Whale Beach is underrated – a paradisaical slice of deep, orange sand flanked by steep cliffs. Caught in a sandy '70s time-warp, Avalon is the mythical Australian beach you always dreamed was there but could never find. When the *Baywatch* producers wanted to film here in the '90s, locals told them to bugger off!

Elongated Narrabeen, immortalised by the Beach Boys in *Surfin' USA*, chases the endless summer south to Collaroy – high-rise apartments and high-rise surf dominate. Distorted from *diwai*, an Aboriginal name for a local bird, Dee Why is a no-fuss family beach with chunky apartments, cafés and *Big Wednesday* breaks.

See p122 for more on Bondi, Bronte and Coogee and p132 for more on Manly.

HIGHLIGHTS

>6 THE ROCKS

SIFT THROUGH THE BONES OF HISTORY IN THE ROCKS
Sydney's first European settlement at The Rocks was a squalid, over-crowded place. Residents sloshed through open sewers; alleyways festered with disease, prostitution and drunken lawlessness.

Shipping services relocated in the 1800s, bubonic plague broke out in 1900, and Harbour Bridge construction in the '20s razed entire streets. It wasn't until the 1970s that The Rocks' cultural and architectural heritage was finally recognised. Redevelopment saved many old buildings, but the area has become an 'olde-worlde' tourist trap. Shops hocking Opera House key-rings proliferate, but gritty history is never far below the surface if you know where to look. Check out Cadman's Cottage (p50), Susannah Place (p52) and the Rocks Discovery Museum (p51). The weekend Rocks Market (p55) is a good excuse to sniff around.

Next door is Millers Point, a low-key colonial district. Garrison Church (1848, Australia's oldest) faces Argyle Place, an English-style village green on which every Australian has the legal right to graze livestock. Nearby, the Lord Nelson Brewery Hotel (p59) and Hero of Waterloo on Windmill St jostle for supreme respect as Australia's oldest pub. Here you'll also find the Sydney Observatory (p52) and the SH Ervin Gallery (p51).

At Walsh Bay you'll find the Sydney Theatre Company (p63), Bangarra Dance Theatre (p59), Sydney Dance Company (p61) and Sydney Theatre (p62).

See also p48.

>7 ROYAL BOTANIC GARDENS

GRAZE THE AFTERNOON AWAY IN THE ROYAL BOTANIC GARDENS

The Royal Botanic Gardens (RBG) were established in 1816 as the colony's veggie patch. The attitude here is relaxed – signs say, 'Please walk on the grass. We also invite you to smell the roses, hug the trees, talk to the birds and picnic on the lawns'. Go exploring, take a free guided walk, or jump on the trackless train if you've outdone yourself.

Highlights include the rose garden, the South Pacific plant collection, the prickly arid garden, the Tropical Centre's glass pyramid and a sinister bat colony (a murder of bats?). Management periodically tries to oust the bats as they destroy the vegetation, but they just keep hanging around…

The gardens' northeastern tip is Mrs Macquaries Point, a functional lookout long before Europeans arrived. It was named in 1810 after Elizabeth, Governor Macquarie's wife, who ordered a chair chiselled into the rock from which she'd view the harbour.

Government House (p50) governs the gardens' northwest sector. The Domain is a large grassy tract linking the RBG and Hyde Park, preserved by Governor Phillip in 1788 for public recreation. The lawns host free summer concerts, Sunday's eccentric Speakers' Corner (p36), and Carols by Candlelight every Christmas. The Art Gallery of NSW (p18) is here, too.

See also p35.

>8 ART GALLERY OF NSW

HANG WITH THE MASTERS AT THE ART GALLERY OF NSW

Playing a prominent and gregarious role in Sydney society is the ultrareputable Art Gallery of NSW. The gallery was established in 1874, when five trustees were appointed to administer a £500 grant from the NSW government towards 'the formation of a gallery of art'. Initially procuring paintings by Sydney and London artists, their vision expanded towards establishing an indigenous collection in the '60s.

Architecturally challenging extensions in the '70s, '90s and 2003 swelled the gallery's ambition further. Today, blockbuster international touring exhibitions arrive regularly (Man Ray, Caravaggio etc), and the gallery houses the world's most broadly representative collection of Australian art.

There are three permanent collections – the European, Australian and Asian Galleries. The controversial Archibald Prize for Australian portraiture exhibits here annually, as do the Wynne Prize (landscape or figure sculpture) and Sulman Prize (subject or mural painting) exhibitions, and the Artexpress exhibition of the year's best Higher School Certificate student art. Kids swarm to the GalleryKids Sunday programme, offering workshops, performances and free guided tours with costumed actors. There are also concerts, screenings, courses, celebrity talks and programmes for the deaf and visually impaired. Speakers' Corner (p36) happens on Sunday afternoons on the lawns out front.

See also p34.

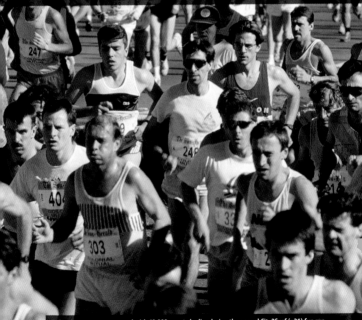

>SYDNEY DIARY

Festivals and events pepper Sydney's social calendar like... well, like pepper. Concert halls and theatres pack 'em in, but it's difficult to keep Sydneysiders inside for long. Sure, locals have season subscriptions to the Sydney Symphony and Sydney Theatre Company, but with so many sunny shores, earnest indoor pursuits often take a back seat.

Sydney's streets are crammed with 60,000 sweaty bodies during the annual City2Surf (p21) fun run.

JANUARY

Sydney Festival
www.sydneyfestival.org.au
Throughout January, Sydney's premiere arts and culture festival expresses itself through musical, stage and street performance, visual art and 'happenings' around town. International and Australian performers swing from opera to water puppetry. Free shows aplenty, plus All Tomorrow's Parties music fest on Cockatoo Island.

Big Day Out
www.bigdayout.com
International music mosh at Sydney Olympic Park. Much head-banging, sun and beer.

Chinese New Year
www.cityofsydney.nsw.gov.au/cny
January/February – food, fireworks, dance, acrobatics, buskers, Chinatown parade and Darling Harbour dragon-boat races.

Flickerfest
www.flickerfest.com.au
International short-film festival at Bondi Pavilion (p123) – shorts, documentaries, animation and workshops. Tours nationally.

FEBRUARY

Gay & Lesbian Mardi Gras
www.mardigras.org.au
A month-long festival and fleshy Oxford St parade. Gyms empty out, solariums

Gawk at the frocked-up and fabulous at Sydney's Gay & Lesbian Mardi Gras darken, waxing emporiums tally profits. And 700,000 people like to watch; after-party tickets are gold.

Tropfest

www.tropfest.com.au

The world's largest short-film festival. Films incorporate a surprise 'signature' prop (kiss, bubble, sneeze etc). Free screenings; celeb judges (David Wenham, Gabriel Byrne, Salma Hayek).

MAY

Australian Fashion Week

www.afw.com.au

Long-legged waifs (of both sexes) strut and pout around Circular Quay. Expect high-profile designers from Australia and the Asia-Pacific region.

Sydney Writers Festival

www.swf.org.au

Readings with social, literary and political writers from Australia and overseas. Not afraid of the big issues; fresh talent abounds.

JUNE

Sydney Biennale

www.biennaleofsydney.com.au

In even-numbered years; international contemporary arts at the Art Gallery of NSW (p18) and city venues.

Go troppo at Tropfest

Darling Harbour International Jazz Festival

www.darlingharbour.com

Free jazzy jamboree. Eclectic artists such as James Morrison, Frank Bennett and the Cat Empire.

Sydney Film Festival

www.sydneyfilmfestival.org

Long-running film fiesta celebrating the human condition; global and local releases.

AUGUST

City2Surf

www.city2surf.com.au

On the second Sunday in August, 60,000 athletes, pretenders and sundry run (or

Head's up! Sculpture by the Sea

National Rugby League (NRL) Grand Final

www.nrl.com.au

The big men collide in the NRL season finale; Aussie Stadium or Telstra Stadium.

NOVEMBER

Sculpture by the Sea

www.sculpturebythesea.com

In mid-November, the clifftop trail from Bondi Beach to Tamarama transforms into a sculpture garden. Serious prize money is on offer for the most creative, curious or quizzical offerings from international and local sculptors.

DECEMBER

Homebake

www.homebake.com.au

A celebration of home-baked Oz Rock talent occupies The Domain in early December.

walk) 14km from Hyde Park to Bondi Beach. The fastest reach the beach in 40 minutes, their athletic seriousness counterbalanced by family fun and the odd cardiac scare.

SEPTEMBER

Sydney Running Festival

www.sydneyrunningfestival.com.au

A once-a-year opportunity to run (or walk) across the Sydney Harbour Bridge to the finish line at the Sydney Opera House.

Festival of the Winds

www.waverley.nsw.gov.au/info
/pavilion/fotw

The second Sunday in September; a multicultural kite-flying fiesta at Bondi Beach.

Sydney to Hobart Yacht Race

www.rolexsydneyhobart.com

On 26 December Sydney Harbour churns with competitors and onlookers for the start of the world's most arduous open-ocean yacht race.

New Year's Eve

www.cityofsydney.nsw.gov.au/nye

Find someone with a penthouse or a yacht to watch the annual fireworks displays over Sydney Harbour. The bridge erupts with pyrotechnic bedazzlement.

Hang out at the Royal Botanic Gardens (p17)

ITINERARIES

If you've only got a day or three to make Sydney's acquaintance, try the following itineraries. Most of Sydney's signature attractions make the grade here, along with some rewarding local hangouts. Alternatively, beat a retreat from the crowds, escape the city on a day trip, or hunt down some free entertainment.

DAY ONE
Ramble down through The Rocks (p16) to Sydney Cove, then out past the Sydney Opera House (p10) to the Royal Botanic Gardens (p17). Grab a cab to Bondi Beach (p122) and dunk yourself in the Pacific. Suitably salted, swill a pre-dinner drink at the Opera Bar (p59), then catch an evening show at the Sydney Opera House (p62). Afterwards, some fresh seafood, divine Australian wine and harbour hubbub at a Circular Quay restaurant (p55) is hard to beat.

DAY TWO
Kick-start your day/heart with a Bridge Climb (p60) over the Sydney Harbour Bridge. Hang with the masters at the Art Gallery of NSW (p34) or ship yourself out onto the harbour: ride the ferry to Taronga Zoo (p134), or to Manly (p132) for a surf or a few hours of beachy empty-headedness. Chug a cold beer at Manly Wharf Hotel (p136), chow-down in Chinatown (p71) then hit some Darlinghurst bars (p104) for a jazzy nightcap.

DAY THREE
Sleep late, caffeinate at Campos (p81), then splash some cash in Paddington's Oxford St boutiques (p113). In the afternoon, make some fishy friends at the Sydney Aquarium (p68) or soar up Sydney Tower (p36) for eye-popping 360-degree views. Head to Darling Harbour for dinner (p71), cool your boots in Cargo Bar (p73), then heat your heels at one of Sydney's hellishly good clubs.

Top left Sharpen your haggling skills at Paddington Market (p116) **Top right** The Opera Bar (p59) provides dinner with a view
Bottom Surfin' Bondi (p131) is the quintessential Sydney experience

FORWARD PLANNING

Three weeks before you go Check out some of the key Sydney websites (p177); get to know what's going on – both in the headlines and after hours – online by reading the local media (p178); check to see if your visit coincides with any major holidays or festivals (p19); make sure your passport and other documents are in order.

One week before you go Book tickets for any major concerts or shows that might interest you at places such as the Sydney Opera House (p62) or the Sydney Theatre Company (p63); book a table at Aria (p55) or Tetsuya's (p43); remind your mother that she promised to feed the cat during your absence.

The day before you go Reconfirm your flight; check the Sydney websites for any last-minute changes or cancellations at entertainment venues; buy some Australian dollars; cancel the milk.

OFF THE BEATEN TRACK

Beat the heat at Balmoral Beach (p15) on the North Shore with some top-notch restaurants and super swimming. At the end of Glebe Point Rd is Jubilee Park (Map p77, B2): snooze in the sun, throw a Frisbee or consume your airport novel under a gargantuan Moreton Bay fig. South of Coogee, oversized Maroubra Beach (p14) has underrated waves and a suburban tempo. West of the madding Rocks is Millers Point (Map p49, B3) where you'll find photogenic terraces, unpretentious pubs and picnic perfection at Sydney Observatory Park (Map p49, B3). Not far from Kings Cross, Rushcutters Bay Park offers uncrowded lawns where the pontoons bump and sway.

FREE STUFF

The Art Galley of NSW is artfully free, while free summer entertainment proliferates with regular musical performances in Sydney's parks. January's Sydney Festival (p20) offers dozens of outdoor events; October's **Manly International Jazz Festival** (www.manly.nsw.gov.au/manlyjazz) and June's Darling Harbour International Jazz Festival (p21) have free outdoor gigs too. The Tropfest (p21) short-film festival in February has free screenings in The Domain and Darlinghurst.

Catch some street theatre and a few buskers at Sydney's weekend markets (p157), or around Circular Quay (p48), Martin Place (p32) or Darling Harbour (p64). The mad, the erudite and the madly erudite vent spleen at Speakers' Corner (p36) on Sunday afternoons. When all else fails, you can't beat a beach and a book (p14).

DAY TRIPPER

Free day up your sleeve? The Sydney Visitor Centre (p180) provides day-trip information.

The **Blue Mountains** (www.visitbluemountains.com.au), 110km west of Sydney, offer jaw-dropping scenery, bushwalks, gorges, gums and gourmet restaurants galore.

Tracking 30km north from Manly (p132), Sydney's sublime **Northern Beaches** (www.sydneybeaches.com.au) feature laid-back 'burbs, gnarly breaks, craggy headlands and fish-and-chip shops.

Ku-ring-gai Chase National Park (www.environment.nsw.gov.au), 24km north of Sydney, has that classic Sydney cocktail of bushland, sandstone and water.

Royal National Park (www.environment.nsw.gov.au), 30km south of the city, features vertiginous cliffs, secluded beaches, coastal scrub, seaside communities and cockatoos.

Parramatta (www.parracity.nsw.gov.au), 24km west of Sydney, was Australia's second European settlement. The town has been subsumed by suburbia, but retains a small-town vibe and a clutch of colonial buildings.

Beautiful Bronte (p122) proves it really is all that

NEIGHBOURHOODS

Central Sydney grips Sydney Harbour (aka Port Jackson) in a passionate embrace. The harbour runs east–west, dividing the city in two – the Sydney Harbour Bridge and Harbour Tunnel connect the south and north shores. The city centre and most of the action is south of the harbour.

Downtown Sydney's flooded with bistros, shops and cool bars that go bump in the night, but the city centre is largely abandoned to the skateboarders on weekends. North of the centre, The Rocks and Circular Quay are tourist meccas with superb restaurants, the Sydney Opera House sitting just northeast of Circular Quay. Southwest of the centre is Chinatown where paper dragons and fireworks temper the shameless restaurant spruikers on Dixon St. Northwest of here is Darling Harbour, an architecturally psychotic tourist haven where boardwalks, museums, restaurants, bars, hotel monoliths and freeway flyovers distract the masses.

The Inner West begins just west of Darling Harbour. Cafés and bookshops tangle with dreadlocked bohemia in Glebe, while grungy Newtown is King of the Inner West – tattoos, tofu and students rule on King St.

South of the city centre, Surry Hills brims with great places to eat and drink and bears absolutely no resemblance to Surrey, England. In Darlinghurst, east of the centre, cafés bulge with cinematographers, thespians and gym-junkies buffing up for Mardi Gras. Infamous Kings Cross stews in its own sleazy, strangely hypnotic brand of sex, drugs and rock 'n' roll. South and west of here, Paddington and Woollahra set Sydney's social high-water mark with avant-garde galleries, gorgeous terrace houses and fabulous boutiques, while everything's pretty in pink along Oxford St, Sydney's gay hub.

Sydney's quintessential ocean suburb is Bondi (surfboards, sushi, internet, beer – take your pick). The eastern beaches track south from Bondi, including family-friendly Bronte and backpacker Coogee.

Across the bridge from The Rocks is the North Shore, the jewel of which is Manly, a beachy, affable 'burb where the surf's as good as the kebabs.

Roseville

Manly
Vale

Chatswood

Castle
Cove

Balgowlah

Willoughby

Manly
MANLY
p133

Lane
Cove

Crows
Nest

The
Spit

Woolwich

North
Sydney

Neutral
Bay

Balmoral

Mosman

Drummoyne

Balmain

Kirribilli

Cremorne
Point

Vaucluse

THE ROCKS &
CIRCULAR QUAY
p49

Leichhardt

Glebe

CITY
CENTRE
p33

CHINATOWN
& DARLING
HARBOUR
pp66-7

KINGS CROSS,
DARLINGHURST
& AROUND pp98-9

Rose
Bay

INNER WEST
p77

SURRY
HILLS
p89

PADDINGTON
& WOOLLAHRA
p111

Double
Bay

Annandale

Redfern

Bondi
Junction

Bondi
Beach

Newtown

Kensington

Bronte

Marrickville

Randwick

BONDI, BRONTE
& COOGEE
pp124-5

SOUTH

Coogee

PACIFIC

OCEAN

Kingsford

Mascot

Botany

Chifley

0 ————————— 3 km
0 ————————— 2 miles

>CITY CENTRE

Sydney's city centre erupts as lunchtime business bods splash cash in the shops and department stores around Pitt St Mall and Martin Pl, and the classy shopping centres along George St. In between purchases they power-lunch at some of the city's most prestigious restaurants. There's a slew of hip, after-work bars here too, many of which slide seamlessly into jazzy, clubby moods later in the night. Clinging to the CBD fringes are some stellar museums, gracious colonial buildings and leafy retreats. The strip of greenery from Hyde Park, undulating through The Domain down to the Royal Botanic Gardens provides a vital counterpoint to the clash and throb of Sydney's commerce; office workers roll up their sleeves, munch falafels and slip off their shoes in the sun. Don't expect much downtown action on weekends though – on Sunday afternoons a sense of desolation weighs down, punctuated only by the occasional tumbleweed rolling through.

CITY CENTRE

🅒 SEE
Art Gallery of NSW 1 D3
Australian Museum 2 C5
Hyde Park Barracks
  Museum 3 C3
Museum of Sydney 4 B1
Parliament House 5 C3
Royal Botanic Gardens ...6 D2
St James Church 7 B3
Stpeakers' Corner 8 D3
Sydney Tower &
  Skywalk 9 B4
Watters Gallery 10 D5

🄷 SHOP
David Jones 11 B4
David Jones 12 B4
Fairfax & Roberts 13 B3
Hobbyco ....(see 19)
Jurlique 14 B4
Kinokuniya 15 A5
Love & Hatred ....(see 23)
Martin & Stein ....(see 19)

Myer 16 A4
Oroton 17 B3
Paspaley Pearls 18 A3
Queen Victoria
  Building 19 A4
Red Eye Records 20 B6
Red Eye Records 21 A3
RM Williams 22 A3
Strand Arcade 23 A3
Strand Hatters ....(see 23)
Tiffany & Co 24 B3
World Square 25 A6

🍽 EAT
Bar Reggio 26 D6
Bécasse 27 A4
Bodhi 28 C4
Est. 29 A2
Forty One 30 C2
Mother Chu's Vegetarian
  Kitchen 31 A6
Prime. 32 B3
Tetsuya's 33 A5

🅈 DRINK
Arthouse 34 A4
Bar Europa 35 B3
Bavarian Bier Café 36 A3
Establishment ....(see 29)
Hemmesphere ....(see 29)
Orbit Lounge Bar 37 A2
Redoak Boutique Beer
  Café 38 A3
Tank Stream Bar 39 B2
Zeta 40 A4

⭐ PLAY
City Recital Hall 41 A3
Crystal Bar 42 A3
Metro Theatre 43 A6
Sydney Architecture
  Walks ....(see 4)
Sydney Conservatorium
  of Music 44 C1
Tank ....(see 39)

A map of central Sydney.

NEIGHBOURHOODS

CITY CENTRE

V

SEE

ART GALLERY OF NSW

☎ 9225 1744; www.artgallery.nsw.gov
.au; Art Gallery Rd, The Domain; admission free, special exhibits vary; ⏱ 10am-
5pm Thu-Tue, to 9pm Wed; 🚇 St James
🚌 441; ♿

Don't miss classic Australian
paintings by Brett Whiteley, Arthur
Streeton, Sidney Nolan and Lloyd
Reese, and the Yiribana Gallery's
Aboriginal and Torres Strait Islander
art. The Sunday GalleryKids activity
programme includes dance, stories,
magic, cartoons and other performances. Tours of the Asian Gallery
with Zhenmu Shou, a ghostly guide
from the grave, are a blast from the
past. See also p18.

The Trade Wall at the Museum of Sydney, located on the site of Sydney's first Government House

○ AUSTRALIAN MUSEUM

☎ 9320 6000; www.amonline.net.au; 6-8 College St; admission $12/6, special exhibits extra; ⊙ 9.30am-5pm; 🚇 Museum Ⓜ Galeries Victoria; ♿

Established just 40 years after the First Fleet dropped anchor, this natural history museum features excellent native wildlife and Aboriginal exhibitions. There are self-guided tours, indigenous performances on Sundays and opportunities for kids to get busy in the Skeleton and Search & Discover galleries.

○ HYDE PARK BARRACKS MUSEUM

☎ 8239 2311; www.hht.net.au; Queens Sq; admission $10/5, introductory room free; ⊙ 9.30am-5pm; 🚇 St James Ⓜ City Centre

Designed by prolific convict architect Francis Greenway, the barracks were used as convict quarters for Anglo-Irish sinners (1819–48), an immigrant depot (1848–86) and government courts (1887–1979) before their current incarnation – a window into everyday convict life. Wheelchair access to ground floor only.

○ MUSEUM OF SYDNEY

☎ 9251 5988; www.hht.net.au; cnr Bridge & Phillip Sts; admission $10/5; ⊙ 9.30am-5pm; 🚇 🚌 ⚓ Circular Quay

Built on the site of Sydney's first (and infamously pungent) Government House, this fragmented, storytelling museum uses state-of-the-art installations to explore the city's people, places, cultures and evolution. Indigenous origins are highlighted, evoking a poetic sense of place. Wheelchair access to ground floor only.

○ PARLIAMENT HOUSE

☎ 9230 2111; www.parliament.nsw .gov.au; Macquarie St; admission free; ⊙ 9am-5pm Mon-Fri; 🚇 Martin Place

Twinned with the Mint building further up Macquarie St, the deep veranda, formal colonnade and ochre tones of Parliament House (1816) define the world's oldest continuously operating parliamentary building. You can watch the elected representatives outdo each other on days when parliament sits. Wheelchair access by private arrangement.

○ ROYAL BOTANIC GARDENS

☎ 9231 8111, Aboriginal Heritage Tours 9231 8134; www.rbgsyd.nsw.gov.au; Mrs Macquaries Rd; admission free, Tropical Centre $5.50/3.30; ⊙ 7am-sunset, Tropical Centre 10am-4pm; 🚇 Circular Quay, Martin Place 🚌 ⚓ Circular Quay; ♿

Free guided walks at 10.30am daily, plus 1pm Monday to Friday from November to March. Aboriginal Heritage Tours ($25/13) depart at 2pm on Friday. There's also a dynamic educational programme of talks and tours, mostly

BATS OUT OF HELL

Cast an eye to the Sydney dusk sky, particularly around the Royal Botanic Gardens, and you'll likely see the silent spectral swoop of a fruit bat on the wing. Actually, calling them bats is a misnomer – they're grey-headed flying foxes *(Pteropus policephalus)*, nocturnal mammals who roost in vast, chattering colonies. Vampire-esque 1m wingspans can make the blood run cold, but don't fret, they'd rather suck on a fig than your jugular.

obsessed with dirt and things that grow in it. Recent highlights have included 'Trees Worth Shouting About' and 'Superscience' sessions. Check the website for details. See also p17.

⊙ ST JAMES' CHURCH

☎ 9232 3022; www.sjks.org.au; 173 King St; admission free; ⏰ 11am-6pm Mon-Fri, 9am-4.30 Sat, 7.30am-4pm Sun; ⊜ St James Ⓜ City Centre

Built from convict bricks, Sydney's oldest church (1819) is another Francis Greenway extravaganza. Originally designed as a courthouse, the brief changed: 'Hey Frank, we need a church!'. The cells became the crypt. Check out the balcony, sparkling copper dome, crypt shop and cool contemporary stained-glass 'Creation Window'.

⊙ SPEAKERS' CORNER

Art Gallery Rd, The Domain; admission free; ⏰ noon-4pm Sun; ⊜ St James ⊞ 441; ♿

Recline on a patch of lawn in front of the Art Gallery of NSW and listen to religious zealots, nutters, political extremists, homophobes, hippies and academics express their earnest opinions. Some of them have something interesting to say; most of them are just plain mad. Either way, it makes for an interesting afternoon. BYO soapbox.

⊙ SYDNEY TOWER & SKYWALK

☎ 9333 9222; www.skywalk.com.au; 100 Market St; admission $24/15, Skywalk $65/45; ⏰ 9am-10.30pm, Skywalk to 10pm; ⊜ St James Ⓜ City Centre; ♿

Sydney Tower is as high as Sydneysiders get without wings or drugs – the 250m-high, 360-degree views are unbeatable. On a clear day you'll see west to the Blue Mountains, south to Botany Bay, east across the harbour to the silvery Pacific and down onto the city streets. Watch rain squalls shift across the suburbs on a stormy day. The tower also has two excellent revolving restaurants – sit and spin above the twinkling harbour city.

Luke Skywalker aspirations? The latest addition to Sydney's big-

Get high on the Sydney Skywalk

ticket tourist checklist is Skywalk: don a spiffy 'skysuit', shackle yourself to the safety rail and step onto two glass-floored viewing platforms outside Sydney Tower's observation deck, high above the street. No place for the weak-bowelled…

WATTERS GALLERY

☎ 9331 2556; www.wattersgallery.com; 109 Riley St, East Sydney; admission free; ☽ 10am-5pm Tue & Sat, 10am-7pm Wed-Fri; 🚇 Museum 🚌 389

Since 1964 this funky institution in the seamy lower reaches of Riley St has been pumping out quality. James Gleeson, Ken Whisson, Tony Tuckson and reformed rock-star Reg Mombassa are just a handful of the iconic Australian artists it holds up to the light.

 SHOP

DAVID JONES
Department Store
☎ 9266 5544; www.davidjones.com.au; cnr Market & Castlereagh Sts; ☽ 9.30am-6pm Mon-Wed, to 9pm Thu, to 7pm Fri, 9am-7pm Sat, 10am-6pm Sun; 🚇 St James, Town Hall Ⓜ City Centre 🚌 George St buses

In two enormous city buildings, David Jones (DJs) is Sydney's premier department store. The Castlereagh St store has women's and children's wear and a friendly concierge to point you in the right direction. Market St has menswear, electrical and a high-brow food court: noses assail chunks of cheese, eyes flutter over antipasto, mouths drool over pastries… Your hip pocket mightn't be as keen on the whole deal as your senses.

HOBBYCO *Toy Shop*
☎ 9264 4877; www.hobbyco.com.au; Shop 50, L2 & L3, Queen Victoria Bldg, 455 George St; ⏰ 10am-6pm Mon-Wed, Fri & Sat, to 9pm Thu, 11am-5pm Sun; 🚇 St James, Town Hall Ⓜ City Centre 🚌 George St buses
Run by hobbyists for people who take toys seriously, Hobbyco's aisles fill with excited boys (big and small) effusing over slot cars, Meccano sets, Hornby trains and radio-controlled cars (such as the kick-arse Audi TT). First Fleet models and 12,000-piece jigsaw puzzles are perfect projects for a rainy year.

JURLIQUE *Cosmetics*
☎ 9232 0626; www.jurlique.com.au; 193 Pitt St Mall; ⏰ 9am-6pm Mon-Wed & Fri, to 8pm Thu, 9am-5.30pm Sat, 11am-5pm Sun; 🚇 St James, Town Hall Ⓜ City Centre 🚌 George St buses
An international success story, the gorgeous, plant-based cosmetics from South Australia's Jurlique are pricey but worth every

face-saving cent. There is another store in **Bondi** (Map p124, D2; ☎ 9365 7715; Shop 1, 36 Campbell Pde) if your skin is a little parched postsurfing.

KINOKUNIYA *Bookshop*
☎ 9262 7996; www.kinokuniya.com; L2, The Galeries Victoria, 500 George St; ⏰ 10am-7pm Mon-Wed, Fri & Sat, to 9pm Thu, 10am-6pm Sun; 🚇 Town Hall Ⓜ Galeries Victoria 🚌 George St buses
Wrapping around the Galeries Victoria atrium, Kinokuniya has more than 300,000 titles – the largest bookshop in Sydney. The comics section is a magnet for geeky teens; the imported Chinese, Japanese and European magazine section isn't. Peruse the music and architecture shelves then hit the café.

LOVE & HATRED *Jewellery*
☎ 9233 3441; www.loveandhatred .com.au; L1, Strand Arcade, 412 George St; ⏰ 10am-5.30pm Mon-Wed & Fri, to 8pm Thu, 10am-4.30pm Sat, 11am-4pm Sun; 🚇 Town Hall Ⓜ City Centre 🚌 George St buses
This plush, sensual, wood-panelled store is aglow with custom-made jewellery by Sydney designer Giovanni D'Ercole. Beautiful sapphire rings, natural pearls and rose-gold pieces manifest an unostentatious, mystic blend of Celtic, Art Nouveau and contemporary styles.

🏛 MYER *Department Store*
☎ 9238 9111; www.myer.com.au; cnr
George & Market Sts; 🕑 9am-7pm
Mon-Wed, Fri & Sat, to 9pm Thu, 10am-
6pm Sun; 🚊 Town Hall Ⓜ City Centre
🚌 George St buses
Formerly the dowdy Grace Bros,
Myer has made a concerted effort
to liven things up a bit. Over seven
floors, there's everything from hip
fashions (Wayne Cooper, Seduce,
Chloe) to big-name cosmetics
(Chanel, Lancôme, Clinique), plus
lingerie, sunglasses and a café.

🏛 OROTON *Fashion*
☎ 9223 2449; www.oroton.com.au;
Shop 1a, 183 Pitt St Mall; 🕑 9am-6pm
Mon-Wed & Fri, to 9pm Thu, 11am-5pm
Sat; 🚊 St James, Martin Place Ⓜ City
Centre 🚌 George St buses
Oroton sells sophisticated leathers
in a select palette of colours: black,
red and tan. Wallets, handbags,
belts, shoes, cufflinks and Jackie
O–style sunglasses all have the air
of instant classics.

🏛 PASPALEY PEARLS *Jewellery*
☎ 9232 7633; www.paspaleypearls
.com.au; 2 Martin Pl; 🕑 10am-5.30pm
Mon-Fri, 10.30am-4pm Sat; 🚊 St James,
Martin Place Ⓜ City Centre 🚌 George
St buses
This shell-shaped store sells lustrous
pearls farmed along uninhabited
coastline from Darwin in the Northern Territory to Dampier in Western

Australia. Classic and modern designs start at $450 for a ring, rising
to more than $1 million for a hefty
strand of perfect pink pearls.

🏛 QUEEN VICTORIA BUILDING *Shopping Centre*
☎ 9265 6869; www.qvb.com.au; 455
George St; 🕑 9am-6pm Mon-Wed & Sat,
to 9pm Thu, 11am-5pm Sun; 🚊 Town Hall
Ⓜ Galeries Victoria 🚌 George St buses
The Queen Victoria Building (QVB)
is a high-Victorian masterpiece oc-
cupying an entire city block. Yeah,
sure, the 200 speciality shops are
great, but check out the wrought-
iron balconies, stained-glass shop-
fronts, mosaic floors, tinkling Baby
Grand and hyper-kitsch animated
Royal Clock (featuring the Battle of
Hastings and hourly beheading of
King Charles I).

🏛 RED EYE RECORDS *Music*
☎ 9299 4233; www.redeye.com.au;
370 Pitt St; 🕑 9am-6pm Mon-Wed &
Fri, to 9pm Thu, to 5pm Sat, 11am-5pm
Sun; 🚊 Museum Ⓜ World Square
🚌 George St buses
Walking into this red-walled rock
'n' roll refuge is like waking up
inside a huge, hung-over eyeball.
The shelves are stocked with a
rampaging collection of classic,
rare and collectable records, crass
rock T-shirts, books, posters and
music DVDs. New music is at the
66 King St branch. Rock-on!

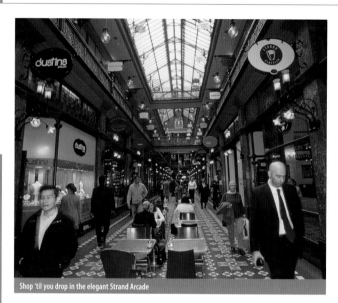
Shop 'til you drop in the elegant Strand Arcade

📷 RM WILLIAMS *Australiana*
☎ 9262 2228; www.rmwilliams.com.
au; 389 George St; ⏱ 8.30am-6pm Mon-
Wed & Fri, to 8.30pm Thu, 9am-5pm Sat,
11am-5pm Sun; 🚆 Town Hall Ⓜ City
Centre 🚌 George St buses
Urban cowboys and country folk
can't get enough of this hard-
wearing outback gear. It's the
kind of stuff politicians don when
they want to seem 'fair dinkum'
about something. Prime ministerial
favourites include oilskin jackets,
Akubra hats, moleskin jeans and
leatherwork boots.

📷 STRAND ARCADE
Shopping Centre
☎ 9232 4199; www.strandarcade.com
.au; 412 George St & 193-5 Pitt St Mall;
⏱ 8.30am-6pm Mon-Wed & Fri, to 8pm
Thu, 9.30am-4pm Sat, 11am-4pm Sun;
🚆 Town Hall Ⓜ City Centre 🚌 George
St buses
Constructed in 1891 in a squeezy
space between George and Pitt Sts,
the Strand Arcade rivals the QVB in
the ornateness stakes. Three floors
of designer fashions, Australiana
and old-world coffee shops are

ALL THAT GLITTERS

Downtown Sydney is a hotspot for stand-out jewellers, comin' atcha like Cleopatra:

> **Fairfax & Roberts** (☎ 9232 8511; www.fairfaxandroberts.com.au; 44 Martin Pl;
  🕙 10am-6pm Mon-Wed & Fri, to 8.30pm Thu, 10.30am-4pm Sat; 🚇 Martin Place)
  Classy, classy, classy... A night at the opera?

> **Martin & Stein** (☎ 9267 6628; www.martinandstein.com.au; Shop 26, QVB, 455 George
  St; 🕙 10am-5pm Mon-Wed & Sat, to 9pm Thu, 11am-5pm Sun; 🚇 Town Hall Ⓜ Galeries Victoria 🚌 George St buses) Objects of virtue, antique jewellery and high security.

> **Tiffany & Co** (☎ 9235 1777; www.tiffany.com; 28 Castlereagh St; 🕙 10am-5pm Mon-
  Wed & Sat, to 7pm Thu, noon-4pm Sun; 🚇 Martin Place) Gorgeous glitterati.

guaranteed to make your short cut through here considerably longer.

Milling around the balconies on level one, top Australian designers commune and collude. Release your inner vixen in low-cut, butt-hugger jeans from **Bettina Liano** (www.bettinaliano.com.au); find devilishly daring gear at **Wayne Cooper** (www.waynecooper.com.au); buy Sydney's best swimwear, hats and suits from **Zimmermann** (www.zimmermannwear.com); and for fish-nets and flounce try **Alannah Hill** (www.alannahhill.com.au).

STRAND HATTERS
Australiana

☎ 9231 6884; www.strandhatters.com.au; Strand Arcade, 412 George St; 🕙 8.30am-6pm Mon-Wed & Fri, to 8pm Thu, 9.30am-4pm Sat, 11am-4pm Sun; 🚇 Town Hall Ⓜ City Centre 🚌 George St buses

Got a cold/wet head? Strand Hatters will cover your crown with a classically Australian Akubra bush hat (made from rabbit felt), a beret, bowler or a Monte Cristo 'Gambler' panama. Staff will block and steam hats to customer requirements (crocodile-teeth hatbands cost extra).

WORLD SQUARE
Shopping Centre

☎ 9262 7926; www.worldsquare.com.au; cnr George & Liverpool Sts; 🕙 10am-7pm Mon-Wed, Fri & Sat, to 9pm Thu, 11am-5pm Sun; 🚇 Town Hall Ⓜ World Square 🚌 George St buses

The old Anthony Horden & Sons department store on this site was demolished in the '80s, and it's taken 20 years for World Square to emerge in its place. City-slickers have been rewarded for their patience with coffee shops, sushi bars, a supermarket, shoe stores and a huge Rebel Sport outlet for every conceivable bat, ball or racket.

🍴 EAT

🍴 BAR REGGIO *Italian* $$

☎ 9332 1129; fax 9332 1129; 135 Crown St, East Sydney; ⏱ 10am-11pm Mon-Fri, to midnight Sat; 🚇 Museum 🚌 389

Blink and you'll miss this classic little dim-lit Italian diner in East Sydney's 'Little Italy' district, a short walk from the CBD. The walls are plastered with Ferrari flags and Rome murals; the menu board in the window has been there so long the lettering has started to flake off. Pasta, pizza, meat and fish dishes have stood the test of time. Closed Sundays (church!).

🍴 BÉCASSE *French* $$$

☎ 9283 3440; www.becasse.com.au; 204 Clarence St; ⏱ noon-2.30pm Mon-Fri, 6.30-10.30pm Mon-Sat; 🚇 Town Hall Ⓜ Galeries Victoria 🚌 George St buses

There's nothing gratuitously flashy about Bécasse, but it will linger as one of the most memorable dining experiences of your trip, the muted, elegant décor perfectly complementing superbly created dishes. The Degustation Menu ($130) is 10 courses of gustatory heaven. Wines by the glass; reservations essential.

🍴 BODHI *Chinese/Vegan* $$

☎ 9360 2523; bodhirestaurant@ bigpond.com; Cook & Phillip Park, 2-4 College St; ⏱ 10am-11pm Tue-Sun,

to 4pm Mon, yum cha 10am-4pm daily; 🚇 Museum, St James; ♿ 🚼 Ⓥ

Bodhi scores highly for its cool design and leafy position. Quick-fire waiters bounce off stainless-steel minimalism inside and slatted wooden tables and umbrellas outside. Have a swim at the pool next door before daily yum cha, a relaxed and value-for-money affair. The barbeque buns rule.

🍴 EST. *Mod Oz* $$$$

☎ 9240 3010; www.merivale.com; L1, Establishment Hotel, 252 George St; ⏱ noon-2.30pm Mon-Fri, 6.30-10.30pm Mon-Sat; 🚇 Circular Quay, Wynyard 🚌 🚢 Circular Quay; ♿

Pressed-tin ceilings, huge columns, oversize windows and modern furniture make Est. a must-see for the interior design as much as the food. Menu stunners include scallops with sauternes and carrot emulsion, and baked baby barramundi. Zealous wine attendants will fetch your desired champagne from the cellar.

🍴 FORTY ONE *Mod Oz* $$$

☎ 9221 2500; www.forty-one.com .au; L42, Chifley Tower, 2 Chifley Sq; ⏱ noon-3pm Tue-Fri, 6-10pm Mon-Sat; 🚇 Martin Place 🚌 George St buses; ♿

Luxury dining with harbour sights and lights – the view extends forever, but the mood remains strangely intimate. It's actually on the 42nd floor, but at this rarefied altitude, most folks are too oxygen-deprived to worry about such details.

🍴 MOTHER CHU'S VEGETARIAN KITCHEN
Vegetarian $

☎ 9283 2828; www.motherchusvegetarian.com.au; 367 Pitt St; 🕐 noon-3pm & 5-10pm Mon-Sat; 🚇 Museum Ⓜ World Square 🚌 George St buses; Ⓥ 👤

Shimmering in plastique splendour beneath the monorail, Mother Chu's blends vegetarian Taiwanese, Japanese and Chinese influences to ensure the perfect tofu or claypot hit. There's not much going on in terms of ambience, but the veg-lovers don't seem to mind.

🍴 PRIME *Steakhouse* $$$

☎ 9229 7777; www.gposydney.com; LG, GPO Bldg, 1 Martin Pl; 🕐 noon-3pm Mon-Fri, 6-10pm Mon-Sat; 🚇 Martin Place 🚌 George St buses; 👤

Need a massive shot of iron? Venture into this carnivores' paradise, deep in a dark, subterranean sandstone bunker. The succulent 400g, aged rib-eye with silky potato purée and a red wine sauce is a protein-packed knockout.

🍴 TETSUYA'S
French/Japanese $$$$

☎ 9267 2900; www.tetsuyas.com; 529 Kent St; 🕐 6-11pm Tue-Fri, noon-3pm

Sat; 🚇 Town Hall Ⓜ World Square 🚌 George St buses

Down a clandestine security driveway, Tetsuya's could well be the ultimate dining experience. Japanese-born Tetsuya Wakuda creates morsels of fusion food with lashings of flavour. You'll find a perfect match for the confit of ocean trout in the 3000-bottle wine cellar. Book way ahead.

🍸 DRINK

🍸 ARTHOUSE *Pub*

☎ 9284 1200; www.thearthousehotel.com.au; 275 Pitt St; admission free; 🕐 11am-midnight Mon-Wed, to 1am Thu, to 3am Fri, 5pm-6am Sat; 🚇 Town Hall Ⓜ Galeries Victoria 🚌 George St buses; 👤

It's easy to lose your way in here, pinballing between three cool bars and the Dome restaurant, staggering through doorways into live jazz performances, dance parties or life-drawing sessions. After-work punters seem to know their way around – follow someone good-looking.

🍸 BAR EUROPA *Bar*

☎ 9232 3377; www.bareuropa.com.au; Basement, 88 Elizabeth St; admission free; 🕐 4pm-late Tue-Fri, 8pm-late Sat; 🚇 Martin Place Ⓜ City Centre

Basement vibe, subtle lighting, DJs spinning laid-back funk and

NEIGHBOURHOODS

CITY CENTRE

three debonair rooms divided by sexy screens cement Europa's reputation as an intimate, clubby hideaway for inner-city professionals. Sip a 'Sydneysider Sour', sigh, and wonder what he/she is doing now…

▼ BAVARIAN BIER CAFÉ
Beer Café

☎ 8297 4111; www.bavarianbiercafe.com.au; 24 York St; admission free; ⏲ 10am-late Mon-Fri, 11am-late Sat; 🚆 Museum Ⓜ World Square 🚌 George St buses

Stepping in the door of this café you'll feel like you've put your head inside an enormous chandelier – sparkling racks of steins dangle above the central bar, waiting for you to fill them with litres of Löwenbrau. Soak it all up with some bratwurst, sauerkraut and a pretzel at the long *bierhalle* tables.

▼ ESTABLISHMENT *Bar*

☎ 9240 3000; www.merivale.com; 252 George St; admission free; ⏲ 11am-late Mon-Fri, 6pm-late Sat; 🚆 Circular Quay, Wynyard 🚌 🚢 Circular Quay; ♿

Establishment's cashed-up crush proves the art of swilling cocktails after a hard, city day is not lost. Sit at the marble bar, in the courtyard or be absorbed by a leather lounge as stockbrokers scribble their phone numbers on the backs of coasters for flirty chicks.

▼ HEMMESPHERE *Bar*

☎ 9240 3040; www.merivale.com; L4, Establishment Hotel, 252 George St; admission free; ⏲ 5.30pm-1am Tue & Wed, to 1.30am Thu, 3pm-2am Fri, 6pm-2am Sat; 🚆 Circular Quay, Wynyard 🚌 🚢 Circular Quay; ♿

This mature, private lounge is pure Sydney opulence; a lush gentlemen's-club vibe peppered with Moroccan twists. Melt into a deep, leather chair, order a cigar and mandarin caipiroska and wait for someone famous to show up. Bookings essential.

▼ ORBIT LOUNGE BAR *Bar*

☎ 9247 9777; www.summitrestaurant.com.au; L47, The Summit, Australia Sq; admission free; ⏲ 5pm-late; 🚆 Wynyard 🚌 George St buses; ♿

A murderously cool, revolving *Goldfinger*-esque bar, orbiting your mind with killer cocktails and views to-die-for. Try the 'D'lux': fresh lychees pureed and shaken silly with Grey Goose orange vodka and Grand Marnier.

▼ REDOAK BOUTIQUE BEER CAFÉ *Beer Café*

☎ 9262 3303; www.redoak.com.au; 201 Clarence St; admission free; ⏲ 11am-10.30pm Mon-Wed, to 1am Thu-Sat; 🚆 Town Hall Ⓜ Darling Park

With more than 20 handmade beers available, this place should keep you off the streets for a

IMPORTANT BEER INFORMATION
Beer in Sydney comes in three glass sizes. Traditional Australian pubs serve the heavenly golden nectar in middys (285mL) and schooners (425mL). Pints (570mL) are the domain of the countless Anglo-Celtic theme pubs that have slipped through quarantine recently. Australian pubs abandoned pints centuries ago because beer would go warm in the summer heat before you'd finished your glass. Arm yourself with this invaluable local insight and order a schooner instead.

while. Pull up a stool among the international crew and work your way through the much-awarded list. If things start to slip away from you, slow your descent with the excellent bar food.

ⓨ TANK STREAM BAR *Bar*
☎ 9240 3000; www.merivale.com; 1 Tank Stream Way; admission free; ⏱ 4pm-midnight Mon-Thu, noon-midnight Fri; 🚉 Circular Quay, Wynyard 🚢 Circular Quay; ♿
After-work suits and secretaries get high and heady poised over Sydney's original water supply. The Tank Stream runs thick with bottled beer, wine and cocktails, and the corporate mob can't get enough. Neither could Robbie Williams.

ⓨ ZETA *Bar*
☎ 9265 6070; www.zetabar.com.au; L4, Hilton Hotel, 488 George St; admission free; ⏱ 5pm-2am Mon-Fri, to 3.30am Sat; 🚉 St James Ⓜ City Centre 🚌 George St buses; ♿
Ride the Hilton escalators up to Zeta, which captivates a chic

young city crew with its white vinyl lounges, discrete curtained booths (exactly what *was* Snoop Dogg smoking in there?) and enormous gas inferno. Here you can sip grilled-fruit cocktails and eyeball the QVB dome from the terrace.

 ## PLAY

☆ CITY RECITAL HALL
Live Music
☎ 8256 2222; www.cityrecitalhall.com; 2-12 Angel Pl; tickets $45-103; ⏱ box office 9am-5pm Mon-Fri; 🚉 Martin Place, Wynyard Ⓜ City Centre 🚌 George St buses; ♿
Based on the classical configuration of the 19th-century European concert hall, the custom-built 1200-seat City Recital Hall boasts near-perfect acoustics. Catch top-flight companies like Musica Viva, the Australian Brandenburg and Chamber Orchestras and the Sydney Symphony as well as touring international ensembles, soloists and opera singers.

NEIGHBOURHOODS

CITY CENTRE

Sydney Philharmonia Motet Choir entertain at the City Recital Hall (p45)

CRYSTAL BAR *Club & Cabaret*
☎ 9229 7799; www.gposydney.com; Lower Level, 1 Martin Pl; admission free-$30; 🕙 5pm-late Wed-Fri, 8pm-late Sat; 🚇 Martin Place

Down in the bowels of the GPO building, Crystal Bar is a lavish, clandestine booze room with smooth-stylin' DJs and 'Crystal Boudoir' – a sassy French knickers-and-high-kicks cabaret show every Saturday night ($30). Who would have thought camp cabaret would appeal to 22-year-olds? Don't you dare dress down.

METRO THEATRE *Live Music*
☎ 9287 2000; www.metrotheatre.com .au; 624 George St; tickets $25-65; 🕙 box office 9am-6pm Mon-Fri, 10am-5pm Sat; 🚇 Town Hall Ⓜ City Centre 🚌 George St buses; ♿

The Metro must be a frontrunner for the 'Sydney's Rockingest Rock Venue' trophy. Big-name indie acts (Stereolab), well-chosen local acts (Josh Pike) and international DJs lend weight to the cause. Theatre-style tiers, air-con, super sound and visibility: r-o-c-k *ROCK!*

SYDNEY ARCHITECTURE WALKS *Organised Tour*
☎ 8239 2211; www.sydneyarchitecture .org; tours depart Museum of Sydney, cnr Bridge & Phillip Sts; tours $25; 🕙 2hr walks, rain or shine

Whoa, who designed *that* gorgeous hacienda/heinous behemoth? These bright young archi-buffs run four themed walking tours: Sydney Opera House, Public Art, Harbour Features & Buildings and Urban Patterns of

Sydney. Call for bookings and departure times.

⭐ SYDNEY CONSERVATORIUM OF MUSIC *Live Music*
☎ 9351 2222; www.music.usyd.edu
.au; cnr Macquarie & Bridge Sts; tickets
free-$25; 🕑 box office 9am-5pm Mon-
Fri; 🚇 Circular Quay, Martin Place
🚌 ⚓ Circular Quay; ♿

'The Con' has a history of bulbous building costs: $145 million was spent recently to refurbish its five venues. The annual student/teacher performance programme includes choral, jazz, operatic and chamber recitals and free lunchtime and 'Cocktail Hour' concerts.

⭐ TANK *Club*
☎ 9240 3007; www.tankclub.com.au;
3 Bridge La; admission Fri/Sat $15/25;
🕑 10pm-6am Fri & Sat; 🚇 🚌 ⚓ Circular Quay

It has a VIP room – the question is, are you 'I' enough? Muster tank-loads of glamour and buckets of chutzpah and crash the party. Otherwise, mingle with *waaay*-too-young, clean-shaven stock-brokers and their waif girlfriends in this world-class, underground club.

>THE ROCKS & CIRCULAR QUAY

Sydney's original European settlement clung to the rocky shelves of The Rocks (www.therocks.com). It was a seedy place, where sailors, whalers and rapscallions boozed and brawled shamelessly in countless harbourside pubs. These days The Rocks is sanitised, touristy and prepackaged, but (thankfully) the historic atmosphere is undeniable. It's an interesting place to wander around for an afternoon, as are Observatory Hill and Millers Point, flanking the western side of the Sydney Harbour Bridge. Sydney's most esteemed theatre and dance companies congregate around Walsh Bay on The Rocks' northern fringe. For more on The Rocks, see p16.

Circular Quay is Sydney's transport hub. The air quality is pretty dire beneath the freeway and railway lines, but around Sydney Cove are some of the city's most esteemed restaurants and, of course, the Sydney Opera House (as if you could miss it). Also here are some impressive museums and galleries, and more bad buskers than you can throw a 5¢ coin at.

THE ROCKS & CIRCULAR QUAY

SEE
Cadmans Cottage 1 D3
Customs House 2 D4
Gannon House 3 C3
Government House 4 F3
Justice & Police Museum ...5 E4
Museum of
  Contemporary Art 6 D3
Original & Authentic
  Aboriginal Art 7 D2
Rocks Discovery
  Museum 8 D3
SH Ervin Gallery 9 B3
Susannah Place 10 C3
Sydney Harbour
  Bridge 11 D1
Sydney Observatory 12 B3
Sydney Opera House ...13 F2

SHOP
Australian Wine Centre ...14 D4
Done Art & Design 15 D3

Sydney Opera House
  Market 16 E2
The Rocks Market 17 D2

EAT
Altitude 18 C3
Aria 19 E3
Bel Mondo 20 C2
Café Sydney ....(see 2)
Cruise 21 D2
Firefly 22 B2
Guillaume at
  Bennelong 23 E2
One Alfred Street 24 D4
Quay 25 D2
Rockpool 26 D3
Sailors Thai
  Canteen 27 D2
The Wharf 28 C1

DRINK
Australian Hotel 29 C3
Blu Horizon ....(see 18)

Lord Nelson Brewery
  Hotel Bistro 30 B2
Opera Bar 31 E2

PLAY
Bangarra Dance
  Theatre ....(see 35)
Bonza Bike Tours 32 C3
BridgeClimb 33 C2
Dendy Opera Quays 34 E3
Sydney Dance
  Company 35 C1
Sydney Ferries
  Cruises 36 D3
Sydney Opera House ...(see 13)
Sydney Theatre 37 B2
Sydney Theatre
  Company 38 C1
The Basement 39 D4
The Rocks Walking
  Tours 40 D2
Whale Watching
  Sydney 41 E3

Farm Cove

Bennelong Point

Sydney Opera House
13
23
10
31

Royal Botanic Gardens

To Opera Air
Cinemas (600m)

Mrs Macquaries Rd

4

Conservatorium Rd

Sydney Harbour Tunnel

Sydney Cove

19
34
41

Circular Quay East

Macquarie St

Albert St
Alfred St
Young St
Phillip St
Bridge St

See City Centre
Map p33

Dawes Point Reserve

Campbells Cove

Dawes Point Park

Park Hyatt

The Rocks
25
21
8
27
32

National Parks & Wildlife Service

Barley & Bligh Reserve

Hickson Rd

George St
17

Suez Canal
26

First Fleet Park
6

Circular Quay

Bus
TransitShop

Loftus St
Reiby Pl
Bulletin Pl

Macquarie Place Park

Pitt St

Dalley St
Gale Pl
Underwood St

24
14

City Host Information
Kiosk (Circular Quay)

Grosvenor St

George St

Harrington St

Essex St

Lang Park

11
Dawes Point

Parbroyal Pier 1

Bradfield Hwy

Lower Fort St

Sydney Visitor Centre
20
30

Gloucester St
35

Cumberland St
18

Cahill Exp

Western Dstr

Piers 2 & 3

Wharf Theatre
28
Piers 4 & 5

Hickson Rd

Dawes Point

Windmill St

Trinity Ave

Watson Rd

Argyle St
Argyle Pl

Bridge
Access Stairs

Sydney Observatory

Observatory Park
Observatory Hill
12

9

22
37
Piers 6 & 7

Piers 8 & 9

Towns Pl

Dalgety Rd

Merriman St
Rhodes La

Munn Street Reserve

Clyne Reserve

Kent St
Argyle La
High La
Lange La
High St
Jenkins St
Hickson Rd

30

Walsh Bay

Millers Point

Millers Point

Sydney Harbour

0   200 m
0   0.1 miles

NEIGHBOURHOODS

THE ROCKS & CIRCULAR QUAY

 # SEE

CADMAN'S COTTAGE
☎ 9247 5033; www.npws.nsw.gov.au;
110 George St, The Rocks; admission free;
🕓 9.30am-4.30pm Mon-Fri, 10am-4.30pm
Sat & Sun; 🚇 🚌 🚢 Circular Quay
Built on a buried beach, Cadman's
Cottage is Sydney's oldest house
(1816). Namesake John Cadman
was Government Coxswain (boat
and crew superintendent). Water
Police detained criminals here in
the 1840s; it was later converted
into a home for retired sea captains.

CUSTOMS HOUSE
☎ 9242 8595; www.cityofsydney.nsw
.gov.au/customshouse; 31 Alfred St,
Circular Quay; admission free; 🕓 8am-
7pm Mon-Fri, 10am-4pm Sat & Sun;
🚇 🚌 🚢 Circular Quay; ♿
Emerging phoenixlike from extensive renovations, this cavernous
harbourside construction (1885)
now houses the Customs House
Library. Under the glass lobby
floor is a charmingly geeky 1:500
model of Sydney; the slick Café
Sydney (p56) is on the roof.

GANNON HOUSE
☎ 9251 4474; www.gannonhouse
gallery.com; 45 Argyle St, The Rocks;
admission free; 🕓 10am-7pm;
🚇 🚌 🚢 Circular Quay
Purchasing works directly from
Aboriginal communities, Gannon

House (named after colonial
builder Michael Gannon) takes an
umbrella approach to its gallery
exhibits, jumbling Aboriginal
artefacts, paintings and didgeridoos with contemporary white
Australian abstract art. The results
are surprisingly harmonious.

GOVERNMENT HOUSE
☎ 9931 5222; www.hht.net.au; admission free; Macquarie St; 🕓 grounds
10am-4pm daily, tours 10.30am-3pm
Fri-Sun; 🚇 Circular Quay, Martin Place
🚌 🚢 Circular Quay
Encased in English-style grounds
within the Royal Botanic Gardens
(p35), this Gothic sandstone mansion has sensational harbour views.
Unless there's an event happening,
you can tour through the fussy
furnishings – look for paintings by
Streeton, Roberts and Drysdale.

JUSTICE & POLICE MUSEUM
☎ 9252 1144; www.hht.net.au; cnr
Albert & Phillip Sts, Circular Quay;
admission $8/4; 🕓 10am-5pm Sat & Sun,
daily in Jan, group bookings Mon-Fri;
🚇 🚌 🚢 Circular Quay
In the old Water Police Station
(1858), this museum adopts the
guise of a late-19th-century police
station and court. Focussing on
disreputable activities, exhibits
include confiscated weapons and
forensic evidence from Sydney's
most heinous crimes. Wheelchair
access to ground floor only.

WORTH THE TRIP
Across the Sydney Harbour Bridge from The Rocks is the famous 1935 amusement park **Luna Park** (☎ 9922 6644; www.lunaparksydney.com; 1 Olympic Pl, Milsons Point; admission free, multiride passes from $20; ⏰ 10am-10pm Sun-Thu, to midnight Fri & Sat; 🚆 🚢 Milsons Point; ♿) with its sinister chip-toothed clown entry. The park has been periodically closed by noise police in recent decades – get in now before it closes again! The Ferris Wheel, Rotor, Flying Saucer and Tumble Bug offer varying degrees of nerve-wrack and nausea.

◉ MUSEUM OF CONTEMPORARY ART
☎ 9245 2400; www.mca.com.au; 140 George St, Circular Quay; admission free; ⏰ 10am-5pm; 🚆 🚌 🚢 Circular Quay; ♿
In a harbourside Art Deco edifice, the MCA has been raising even the most open-minded Sydney eyebrows since 1991. Constantly changing controversial exhibitions from Australia and overseas range from incredibly hip to in-your-face, sexually explicit and profoundly disturbing. Impressive.

◉ ORIGINAL & AUTHENTIC ABORIGINAL ART
☎ 9251 4222; www.authaboriginalart .com.au; 79 George St, The Rocks; admission free; ⏰ 10am-6pm; 🚆 🚌 🚢 Circular Quay
This trustworthy gallery specialises in works from four specific regions – the Central and Western Deserts, Queensland, Arnhem Land and the Kimberleys – with info available on the artists, and some more unusual stuff for sale such as painted glass

and traditional sand paintings preserved on canvas.

◉ ROCKS DISCOVERY MUSEUM
☎ 9240 8680; www.rocksdiscovery museum.com; 2-8 Kendall La, The Rocks; admission free; ⏰ 10am-5pm; 🚆 🚌 🚢 Circular Quay
Divided into four displays (pre-1788, 1788–1820, 1820–1900 and 1900–present) this excellent museum digs deep into The Rocks history and leads you on an arte-fact-soaked tour. Sensitive attention is given to The Rocks' original inhab itants, the Cadigal people. Wheel-chair access to ground floor only.

◉ SH ERVIN GALLERY
☎ 9258 0173; www.nationaltrust.com. au/placestovisit/sheg/; National Trust Centre, Observatory Hill, Watson Rd, The Rocks; admission $7/5; ⏰ 11am-5pm Tue-Sun; 🚆 🚢 Circular Quay 🚌 339, 431-4; ♿
High on the hill inside a former mili-tary hospital and high school, the SH Ervin Gallery exhibits invariably

rewarding historical and contemporary Australian art. Annual mainstays include the 'Salon des Refuses' (alternative Archibald Prize entries), 'The Year in Art' and the 'Portia Geach Memorial Award'.

🄲 SUSANNAH PLACE
☎ 9241 1893; www.hht.net.au; 58-64 Gloucester St, The Rocks; admission $8/4; 🕙 10am-5pm Sat & Sun, daily Jan; 🚆 🚌 🚢 Circular Quay

Dating from 1844, the typically claustrophobic Susannah Place is a diminutive terrace of tiny houses with a tiny shop selling tiny historical wares. My, haven't we grown?

🄲 SYDNEY HARBOUR BRIDGE
☎ 9240 1100; www.pylonlookout.com.au; museum admission $9.50/4; 🕙 10am-5pm; 🚆 🚌 🚢 Circular Quay, Milsons Point

Climb the 200 stairs inside the southeast pylon of the iconic Sydney Harbour Bridge (see p11) and check out the museum. Three levels of exhibits focus on the bridge's planning and construction, and the uncompromising vision of chief engineer JJC Bradfield. And the view is pretty sweet! The entrance is on the pedestrian walkway across the bridge, accessed via the stairs from Cumberland St, The Rocks, or Milsons Point train station, on the North Shore. If you'd like to

COAT-HANGER COMPENDIUM
Out-nerd your mates with a fistful of Harbour Bridge stats:
> The old coat-hanger is 134m high, 502m long and 49m wide
> 1400 workers took nine years to build it
> 16 builders died in construction accidents
> A full makeover takes 10 years and 30,000L of paint
> It weighs nearly 53,000 tonnes
> Six million bolts hold it together; a mythical solid-gold rivet somewhere on the bridge remains elusive

clamber on the bridge itself, see BridgeClimb, p60.

🄲 SYDNEY OBSERVATORY
☎ 9921 3485; www.sydneyobservatory.com.au; Observatory Hill, Watson Rd, The Rocks; admission free, 3-D Space Theatre $7/5, Night Viewings $15/10; 🕙 10am-5pm, 3-D Space Theatre 2.30 & 3.30pm Mon-Fri, 11am & noon Sat & Sun; 🚆 🚢 Circular Quay 🚌 339, 431-4

Built in the 1850s, Sydney's copper-domed, Italianate observatory squats atop Observatory Hill. Inside is Australia's oldest working telescope (1874), a 3-D Space Theatre and an interactive Australian Astronomy exhibition of Aboriginal sky stories and modern stargazing. Squint at galaxies far, far away during Night Viewings

NEIGHBOURHOODS

THE ROCKS & CIRCULAR QUAY

Be dazzled by the heavenly curves of the Sydney Opera House

(bookings required). If you're feeling more earthly, Observatory Park is great for a terrestrial picnic.

☉ SYDNEY OPERA HOUSE

☎ 9250 7111, box office 9250 7777, tours 9250 7250; www.sydneyopera house.com; Bennelong Pt, Circular Quay East; building admission free, performances $25-220; ⏲ box office 9am-8.30pm Mon-Sat, 2hr preshow Sun; 🚊 🚌 ⚓ Circular Quay; ♿
A one-hour tour of Sydney's fabulous Opera House costs $35 for

adults, $24.50 concession, departing half-hourly from 9am to 5pm. A 90-min tour ($150) at 7am daily takes people to see most things behind-the-scenes. Also running is the 'Kids at the House' programme, featuring kids' music, dance and drama including introductory ballet with Australian Ballet dancers. The free bimonthly *Events* diary has upcoming listings; the Sydney Opera House Market (p54) happens on Sunday. See also p10, and p62 for entertainment options.

NEIGHBOURHOODS

THE ROCKS & CIRCULAR QUAY

SHOP

AUSTRALIAN WINE CENTRE
Food & Drink

☎ 9247 2755; www.australianwinecentre.com; Shop 3, Goldfields House, 1 Alfred St, Circular Quay; 🕙 9.30am-6.30pm Mon-Sat, 11am-5pm Sun; 🚻 🚌 🚉 Circular Quay

This multilingual basement store is packed full of quality Australian wine, beer and spirits. Pick up some Yellowglen for a bubbly night or organise a shipment of Ninth Island Pinot Noir back home. Healthy wallets can access Cuban cigars and a swaggering range of Penfolds Grange wines.

DONE ART & DESIGN
Australiana

☎ 9251 6099; www.done.com.au; 123-5 George St, The Rocks; 🕙 10am-6pm; 🚻 🚌 🚉 Circular Quay

Ken Done is like George Michael – he peaked in the '80s but he just won't go away. The sunny side of Australiana, his optimistic, colourful images of Sydney icons are primed for the tourist market. They're emblazoned on everything from T-shirts to handbags. Strewth Ken, not another Opera House mouse-pad…

SYDNEY OPERA HOUSE MARKET *Market*

☎ 9315 7011; www.blueskymarkets.com.au/soh.html; Sydney Opera House, Bennelong Pt, Circular Quay East; 🕙 9am-4pm Sun; 🚻 🚌 🚉 Circular Quay

Under big, cream umbrellas and Opera House arcs, elbow for position in the hunt for high-quality contemporary Australian ceramics,

Shop beneath the sails at The Rocks Market

gems, toys, jewellery, hats, paintings, photographs and souvenirs. If the 40 stalls don't satisfy, just dig the architecture.

⬛ THE ROCKS MARKET Market
☎ 9240 8717; www.therocksmarket .com; George St, The Rocks, near Sydney Harbour Bridge; 🕑 10am-5pm Sat & Sun; 🚇 🚌 ⛴ Circular Quay
The promoter's line goes, 'Choose something you like, somewhere you love'. Under a long white canopy, the 150 stalls here are a little on the tacky side of the tracks (fossils, opals, faux-Aboriginal art etc) but are still worth a gander. Maybe what you choose to like will be the buskers and a beer at the pub.

🍴 EAT

🍴 ALTITUDE Mod Oz $$$
☎ 9250 6123; www.shangri-la.com /sydney; L36, Shangri-La Hotel, 176 Cumberland St, The Rocks; 🕑 6pm-late Mon-Sat; 🚇 🚌 ⛴ Circular Quay; ♿
Superchef Steven Krasicki plates up top-notch Mod Oz at Altitude, sending your taste buds soaring as high as the harbour views. If you've only got a day or two in Sydney, make this your last hurrah.

🍴 ARIA Modern European $$$$
☎ 9252 2555; www.ariarestaurant .com; 1 Macquarie St, Circular Quay East;

WORTH THE TRIP
Perched above the North Sydney Olympic Pool just across the bridge from The Rocks is superslick **Aqua Dining** (☎ 9964 9998; www.aquadining .com.au; cnr Paul & Northcliff Sts, Milsons Pt; 🕑 noon-2.30pm & 6-10pm; 🚇 ⛴ Milsons Point; ♿ Ⓥ). Muted mushroom hues play second-fiddle to bridge and harbour views, while the service is superior – that rare mix of courteous, knowledgeable (the wine list beggars belief) and amiable. Put your hand up for the saddle of lamb.

🕑 noon-3pm Mon-Fri, 5.30-11pm Mon-Sun; 🚇 🚌 ⛴ Circular Quay; ♿
Aria is a star in Sydney's fine-dining firmament, an award-winning combination of chef Matthew Moran's stellar dishes, awesome Opera House views (is there a cooler building?) and faultless service. The mouth-watering lamb rack is hard to overlook. Pre- and after-theatre supper menu available.

🍴 BEL MONDO Italian $$$
☎ 9241 3700; www.belmondo .com.au; L3, Argyle Stores, Gloucester Walk, The Rocks; 🕑 noon-4pm Fri, 6-10pm Tue-Sat; 🚇 🚌 ⛴ Circular Quay; ♿
Expect northern Italian cuisine perfectly executed by chef Andy

NEIGHBOURHOODS

THE ROCKS & CIRCULAR QUAY

Bull in dramatic surrounds – space, views, elegance and pizzazz; *very* Sydney. For a more relaxed meal, the cool and casual bar is perfect for an after-work bite or a late-night supper.

🍴 CAFÉ SYDNEY *Mod Oz* $$$

☎ 9251 8683; www.cafesydney .com; L5, Customs House, Circular Quay; 🕐 noon-11pm Mon-Fri, 5-11pm Sat, noon-4pm Sun; 🚇 🚌 ⛴ Circular Quay; ♿ 🚼 V

A roomy dining hall on the Customs House roof with outrageous harbour views, outdoor terrace, glass ceiling, cocktail bar, friendly staff, Sunday afternoon jazz and superchef Nino Borgo; the list of Café Sydney's pluses is as long as your arm. Seafood and wood-grilled dishes prevail.

🍴 CRUISE *Mod Oz* $$$

☎ 9251 1188; www.cruisebar.com .au/restaurant; L2, Overseas Passenger Terminal, Circular Quay West; 🕐 noon-3pm Wed-Fri, 6pm-late Tue-Sun; 🚇 🚌 ⛴ Circular Quay; ♿ V

The cocktail lounge upstairs wallows in lugubrious style; the bar downstairs does a heady trade. In between, Cruise restaurant cooks up satisfying serves of prawn-and-scallop dumplings with red vinegar, and local snapper fillet with shaved fennel, prawns and tomato vinaigrette. Tasty work.

🍴 FIREFLY *Tapas & Wine Bar* $$

☎ 9241 2031; www.fireflybar.net; Lot 5, Pier 7, 17 Hickson Rd, Walsh Bay, The Rocks; 🕐 noon-11pm Mon-Sat; 🚇 ⛴ Circular Quay 🚌 430-4; ♿ V

Compact, classy and never snooty, Firefly's outdoor candlelit tables fill with pretheatre patrons having a quick meal before the show. Come after 8pm when the audience has taken its seats and toast the Walsh Bay powerboats with some fine wine.

🍴 GUILLAUME AT BENNELONG *Mod Oz & French* $$$$

☎ 9241 1999; www.guillaumeatbe nnelong.com.au; Sydney Opera House, Bennelong Pt, Circular Quay East; 🕐 noon-3pm Thu & Fri, 5.30pm-late Mon-Sat; 🚇 🚌 ⛴ Circular Quay; ♿ V

Turn the old 'dinner and a show' cliché into something meaningful at the Sydney Opera House. Snuggle into a banquette and enjoy acclaimed chef Guillaume Brahimi's masterful cuisine. His basil-infused tuna with mustard seed and soy vinaigrette has fans hollering operatically all over town.

🍴 ONE ALFRED STREET *Café & Wine Bar* $$

☎ 9241 4636; onealfredst@bigpond .com; 1 Alfred St, Circular Quay; 🕐 8am-

late, kitchen noon-9pm;
🚃 🚌 ⛴ Circular Quay; ♿ Ⓥ
An unexpected gem among the morass of Circular Quay fast-food joints, One Alfred Street serves up classics such as slow-cooked Wagyu beef with potato and parsnip flakes and quality fish and chips. Also great for a morning caffeine fix or a lazy afternoon vino (Antipodean wines only!).

🍴 QUAY Mod Oz $$$
☎ 9251 5600; www.quay.com.au; L3, Overseas Passenger Terminal, Circular Quay West; 🕐 noon-2.30pm Tue-Fri, 6-10pm daily; 🚃 🚌 ⛴ Circular Quay; ♿ Ⓥ
With iconic Sydney on view, sitting on the balcony next to the teary, streamer-hurling non-embarkers at the Overseas Passenger Terminal is surreal. Equally euphoric is Quay's stylish service, outstanding wine list and Peter Gilmore's cooking (try the poached quail with truffle custard, radish, sherry reduction and baked milk skin).

🍴 ROCKPOOL Mod Oz $$$$
☎ 9252 1888; www.rockpool.com; 107 George St, The Rocks; 🕐 6-11pm Tue-Sat; 🚃 🚌 ⛴ Circular Quay; Ⓥ
Behind an unassuming green façade, Rockpool is arguably Sydney's best restaurant (oh, how they argue). Chef Neil Perry's

modern seafood creations continue to wow the critics – expect crafty, contemporary cuisine with Asian influences, faultless service and an alluring wine list. Try Perry's signature stir-fried mud crab omelette.

🍴 SAILORS THAI CANTEEN
Thai $$
☎ 9251 2466; www.sailorsthai.com.au; 106 George St, The Rocks; 🕐 noon-10pm Mon-Sat; 🚃 🚌 ⛴ Circular Quay; Ⓥ ♿
Wedge yourself into a gap between arts-community operators, politicians and media manoeuvrers at Sailors' long communal table and order the Chiang Mai chicken curry. The balcony tables fill up fast, but fortune might be smiling on you.

🍴 THE WHARF Mod Oz $$$
☎ 9250 1761; www.thewharf restaurant.com.au; Pier 4, Hickson Rd, Walsh Bay, The Rocks; 🕐 noon-3pm & 6pm-late Mon-Sat; 🚃 ⛴ Circular Quay 🚌 430-4
Picture-postcard views, sexy staff and photo-worthy Mod Oz – the Wharf has it all on tap, but manages to remain unpretentious and grounded. Perfect for a romantic occasion (such as your holiday), or a pre- or post-theatre drink or bite. One of our favourites.

DRINK

▼ AUSTRALIAN HOTEL Pub

☎ 9247 2229; www.australianheritage hotel.com; 100 Cumberland St, The Rocks; admission free; ◷ 11am-midnight Mon-Sat, to 10pm Sun; ▤ ▤ ▲ Circular Quay

This laid-back, good-humoured hotel has an astounding 96 Australian brews on offer. Try to think of four more to hit the century as you wobble through the list. The pub food borders on gourmet, and you can also sleep upstairs if you've had a few too many.

▼ BLU HORIZON Bar

☎ 9250 6000; www.shangri-la.com /sydney; L36, Shangri-La Hotel, 176 Cumberland St, The Rocks; admission free; ◷ 5pm-late Sun-Thu, 3pm-late Fri, noon-late Sat; ▤ ▤ ▲ Circular Quay; ♿

Look, George Clooney's skinny-dipping in the Park Hyatt roof pool! If you can tear your eyes away, the horizon is indeed blue, the views stretching from here to New Zealand. Can you believe there are 300 cocktails at the bartenders' disposal? Believe it.

Sample some of the 96 Aussie beers on offer at the Australian Hotel, The Rocks, Sydney.

RESPONSIBLE SERVING OF ALCOHOL

Pub cellars at The Rocks were regularly used as impromptu holding cells for passed-out boozers. After emptying their customers' pockets, publicans would dutifully pour drunks down their coal chutes to sleep off the grog in peace. These dank sandstone pits witnessed many a foul hangover, sometimes also harbouring escaped convicts and crims on the run.

☿ LORD NELSON BREWERY HOTEL *Pub*

☎ 9251 4044; www.lordnelson.com.au; 19 Kent St, Millers Point; admission free; ⏰ 11am-11pm Mon-Sat, noon-10pm Sun; 🚇 Circular Quay 🚌 339, 431-4
Built in 1841, the 'Nello' claims to be Sydney's oldest pub (or is it the Hero of Waterloo down the road?) The on-site brewery cooks up robust stouts and ales (try the 'Nelson's Blood') and there's decent midrange accommodation upstairs too.

☿ OPERA BAR *Bar*

☎ 9247 1666; www.operabar.com.au; Lower Concourse, Sydney Opera House, Bennelong Pt, Circular Quay East; admission free; ⏰ 11am-late; 🚇 🚌 ⛴ Circular Quay; ♿
Lapping on the harbour's edge under the low-slung Opera House eaves, this sexy, curvilinear room

grabs everyone from snap-happy tourists to business lunchers and tutors them in the ways of sophisticated boozing. DJs play jazz, soul and funk nightly; bridge views play 24/7.

⭐ PLAY

BANGARRA DANCE THEATRE *Dance*

☎ 9251 5333; www.bangarra.com.au; Pier 4 & 5, Hickson Rd, Walsh Bay, The Rocks; tickets $20-50; ♿ ♿
Bangarra is hailed as Australia's finest Aboriginal dance company. Artistic director Stephen Page conjures a fusion of contemporary themes and indigenous traditions, blending Torres Strait Islander dance with Western technique. Often performing at the Sydney Opera House; bookings essential.

☆ BONZA BIKE TOURS *Organised Tour*

☎ 9331 1127; www.bonzabiketours .com; 30 Harrington St, The Rocks ; tours $89/69; ⏰ 10.30am; 🚇 🚌 ⛴ Circular Quay
These bonza bike boffins run daily 3½-hour 'Sydney Classic' bike tours – a great introduction to the harbour city, trundling past the Opera House, Hyde Park, Darling Harbour, Chinatown, Sydney Tower and the Royal Botanic Gardens. Ask about Manly and Sydney Highlights tours.

THE ROCKS & CIRCULAR QUAY

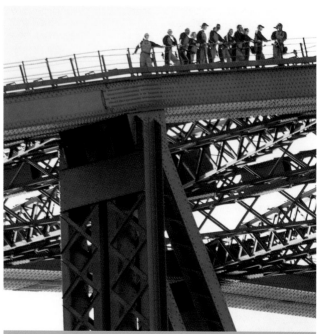

Conquer the dizzying heights of the city's great bridge on the famous Bridge Climb

⭐ BRIDGECLIMB *Activity*

☎ 8274 7777; www.bridgeclimb.com; 5 Cumberland St, The Rocks; tours normal/peak $179/295; 🚌 🚃 🚢 Circular Quay

Once only painters and daredevils (including your author!) scaled the Harbour Bridge heights, but these days anyone can do it. Make your way through the departure lounge and extensive training session, don your headset, umbilical cord and dandy grey jumpsuit (Elvis would be so proud) and up you go. The 3½-hour tours run around the clock and there are two climbs to choose from: the famous Bridge Climb, and the Discovery Climb – less about the view and 'personal achievement', more about the nuts, bolts and internal workings.

★ DENDY OPERA QUAYS
Cinema

☎ 9247 3800; www.dendy.com.au; Shop 9, 2 Circular Quay East; tickets $14.50/10; ✆ 10am-9pm; 🚇 🚌 ⛴ Circular Quay; ♿
When the harbour glare and squawking seagulls get too much, duck into the dark folds of this plush cinema, screening first-run, independent world films, augmented by friendly attendants, a café and a bar. There's also the **Dendy Newtown** (Map p77, B5; ☎ 9550 5699; 261-3 King St).

★ NIGHT CAT TOURS
Organised Tour

Map p124, A3; ☎ 1300 551 608; www.nightcattours.com; 8/137 Bronte Rd, Bondi Junction, hotel pick-ups available; tours $75; ✆ 6.30-10pm Mon, Wed, Fri & Sat
Experience the good, the bad and the ugly of nocturnal Sydney with a small-group tour through the city, Balmain, McMahons Point, Woolloomooloo and Kings Cross. The tour includes two drinks and dinner – a salubrious 'Tiger' pie at Harry's Café de Wheels (p103).

★ SYDNEY DANCE COMPANY
Dance

☎ 9258 4818; www.sydneydancecompany.com; Pier 4 & 5, Hickson Rd,

Walsh Bay, The Rocks; tickets $29-69; 🚇 ⛴ Circular Quay 🚌 430-4; ♿
Australia's No 1 contemporary dance company has been lubricating the nation's cultural psyche for more than 25 years, staging wildly modern, sexy, sometimes shocking works. Inexhaustible artistic director Graeme Murphy retired in 2007 (he got tired), but the SDC hasn't dropped the ball. Dance lessons from the pros are just $18!

★ SYDNEY FERRIES
Self-guided Tour

☎ 9246 8363, 131 500; www.sydneyferries.info; Circular Quay; tickets from $5.20; ✆ 6am-midnight; 🚇 🚌 ⛴ Circular Quay; ♿
If anyone's got the credentials to show you Sydney Harbour, it's Sydney Ferries. Jump on an

The city lights up for Sydney Ferries

old slow-boat to Manly, Mosman, Neutral Bay, Watsons Bay, Balmain, Darling Harbour or anywhere that takes your fancy and enjoy the cheapest Sydney Harbour tour on offer!

🌟 SYDNEY OPERA HOUSE
Theatre & Live Music & Dance
☎ 9250 7777; www.sydneyoperahouse .com; Bennelong Pt, Circular Quay East; performances $25-220; ✆ box office 9am-8.30pm Mon-Sat, 2hr preshow Sun; 🚌 🚢 Circular Quay; ♿
When it's not admiring itself in the mirror, the Opera House regularly hosts the **Australian Ballet** (☎ 1300 369 741; www.australianballet .com.au), **Australian Chamber Orchestra** (☎ 8274 3800; www.aco.com.au), Bangarra Dance Theatre (p59), **Bell Shakespeare** (☎ 8298 9000; www .bellshakespeare.com.au), **Musica Viva** (☎ 8694 6666; www.mva.org.au), **Opera Australia** (☎ 9699 1099; www.opera -australia.org.au), the Sydney Dance Company (p61), **Sydney Philharmonic Choirs** (☎ 9251 2024; www .sydneyphilharmonia.com.au), **Sydney Symphony** (☎ 8215 4600; www .sydneysymphony.com) and the Sydney Theatre Company (opposite). Phew…

🌟 SYDNEY THEATRE *Theatre*
☎ 9250 1999; www.sydneytheatre .org.au; 2 Hickson Rd, Walsh Bay, The Rocks; tickets $69-130; ✆ box office

9am-8.30pm Mon-Sat, 3-5.30pm Sun performance days; ☎ 🚇 **Circular Quay** 🚌 **430-4;** ♿
Opening a few years ago with a name it seems odd no-one thought of before, the resplendent Sydney Theatre at the base of Observatory Hill puts 850 bums on seats for specialist drama and dance.

⭐ **SYDNEY THEATRE COMPANY** *Theatre*
☎ 9250 1777; www.sydneytheatre.com .au; Pier 4 & 5, Hickson Rd, Walsh Bay, The Rocks; tickets $20-130; ⏱ box office 9am-8.30pm, from 11am Sat; ☎ 🚇 Circular Quay 🚌 430-4; ♿
Working in tandem with the Sydney Theatre across the road, the STC is Sydney's premier theatre company. Major Australian actors (Barry Otto, Deborah Mailman) perform works by Alan Bennett, David Williamson and Shakespeare; smaller works play the Wharf, bigger shows play the Sydney Theatre and Opera House. Ask about $20 'Student Rush' tickets.

⭐ **THE BASEMENT** *Live Music*
☎ 9251 2797; www.thebasement.com .au; 29 Reiby Pl, Circular Quay; tickets from $15; ⏱ noon-1.30am Mon-Thu, to 2.30am Fri, 7.30pm-3am Sat, 7pm-1am Sun; ☎ 🚌 🚇 Circular Quay
Sydney's premier jazz venue presents big touring acts (Taj

Mahal, Richard Buckner) and big local talent (Vince Jones, Mia Dyson). A broad musical mandate also sees funk, blues and soul bands performing plus the odd spoken-word gig. Avoid the standing-room-only bar; book a table by the stage.

⭐ **THE ROCKS WALKING TOURS** *Organised Tour*
☎ 9247 6678; www.rockswalkingtours .com.au; 23 Playfair St, The Rocks; tours $30/15; ⏱ 10.30am, 12.30pm & 2.30pm Mon-Fri, 11.30am & 2pm Sat & Sun; ☎ 🚌 🚇 Circular Quay; 🚶
Ninety-minute tours of the historic Rocks that both entertain and exercise. These guys have been around since 1978, so they know The Rocks like the back of their hand(s).

⭐ **WHALE WATCHING SYDNEY** *Organised Tour*
☎ 9583 1199; www.whalewatchingsyd ney.net; Eastern Pontoon, Circular Quay East; tours $85/15; ⏱ 9.45am & 1pm May-Dec; ☎ 🚌 🚇 Circular Quay; 🚶
Humpback and Southern Right whales habitually shunt up and down the Sydney coastline, sometimes venturing into the harbour (p168). Whale Watching Sydney runs three-hour seasonal tours with a 98% sighting success rate! Tours also depart Cockle Bay Wharf, Darling Harbour, 30 minutes prior to Circular Quay.

>CHINATOWN & DARLING HARBOUR

Sandwiched between the city centre and Darling Harbour, Sydney's Chinatown is a tight nest of restaurants, shops and aroma-filled alleyways around Dixon St. Food is what you're here for: top-notch Chinese, $5 food-court noodles and weekend yum cha. Shopping in Chinatown is fun too – whether you're on the scent of some incense, or tracking down a pseudo-Prada bag, the latest MP3 player or Hong Kong martial arts DVD, you'll find it here. Dipping into the hypercommerce of Paddy's Markets is an essential Chinatown experience.

Darling Harbour (www.darlingharbour.com) is a rambling, purpose-built tourist park lining Cockle Bay on the city's western edge. Dotted between an architectural spoil of flyovers, fountains, sculptures and sailcloth are some great museums. The snazzy Cockle Bay Wharf and King Street Wharf precincts contain a dangerous array of cafés, bars and restaurants for when you're all museumed-out. Beneath the flocks of tourists and belligerent ibises, the harbour itself remains unflappably placid.

CHINATOWN & DARLING HARBOUR

◉ SEE
Australian National
   Maritime Museum 1 B2
Chinese Garden of
   Friendship 2 D5
City Rail Information
   Booth 3 E8
Powerhouse Museum 4 C6
Sydney Aquarium 5 C3
Sydney Wildlife World ...6 C2

▢ SHOP
Cyril's Fine Foods 7 E6
Good Living Growers'
   Market 8 B2

Paddy's Markets 9 D6
Ultimo Wine
   Centre 10 B6

▥ EAT
BBQ King 11 D5
Blackbird 12 C4
Bungalow 8 ....13 C1
Chinatown Noodle
   Restaurant 14 D7
Chinta Ria, Temple of
   Love 15 D3
Golden Century 16 D6
Xic Lo 17 D7
Zaaffran 18 C3

▸ DRINK
Cargo Bar 19 C2
The Loft 20 C1

★ PLAY
Home 21 C4
James Craig 22 B1
Slip Inn 23 D2
Sydney by Sail 24 C3
Sydney Entertainment
   Centre 25 D6

Please see over for map

◉ SEE

◉ AUSTRALIAN NATIONAL MARITIME MUSEUM
☎ 9298 3777; www.anmm.gov.au; Darling Harbour; admission free, special exhibits from $10/6; ⏱ 9.30am-5pm; 🚇 Town Hall Ⓜ Harbourside 🚌 🛳 Pyrmont Bay; ♿

Beneath an Utzonlike roof, the Maritime Museum sails through Australia's inextricable relationship with the sea. Exhibitions range from Aboriginal canoes to surf culture and the navy. You can almost taste the salt.

◉ CHINESE GARDEN OF FRIENDSHIP
☎ 9281 6863; www.chinesegarden .com.au; Darling Harbour; admission $6/3; ⏱ 9.30am-5pm; 🚇 Town Hall Ⓜ Garden Plaza 🚌 Exhibition Centre 🛳 Darling Harbour; ♿

Built according to the balanced principles of Yin and Yang, the Chinese Garden of Friendship is an oasis of tranquillity. Designed by architects from Guangzhou (Sydney's sister city) for Australia's bicentenary in 1988, the garden interweaves pavilions, waterfalls, lakes and paths – too

Learn about salt, sand and sails at the Australian National Maritime Museum

serene for words (so shut-up and be still).

☻ POWERHOUSE MUSEUM
☎ 9217 0111; www.powerhousemu seum.com; 500 Harris St, Ultimo; admission $10/6, special exhibits extra; ⏲ 10am-5pm; Ⓜ Powerhouse Museum 🚌 Haymarket 🚌 501 from Town Hall; ♿
A short walk from Darling Harbour, Sydney's hippest and most progressive museum whirrs away inside the former power station for Sydney's defunct tram network. High-voltage interactive demonstrations wow school groups with the low-down on how lightning strikes, magnets grab and engines growl.

☻ SYDNEY AQUARIUM
☎ 8251 7800; www.sydneyaquarium .com.au; Aquarium Pier, Darling Harbour; admission $32/22.50, Aquarium Pass incl admission & return ferry from Circular Quay $33/17; ⏲ 9am-10pm, last admission 9pm; 🚌 Town Hall Ⓜ Darling Park

Satisfy your inner geek at the Powerhouse Museum

NEIGHBOURHOODS

CHINATOWN & DARLING HARBOUR

SHARKY
Shark-o-phobia getting you down? A recent survey found that four species have been responsible for around 100 Sydney shark attacks since 1791: Oceanic White Tip, Great White, Tiger and Bull sharks. Attacks peaked between 1920 and 1940, but since shark net installation began in 1937 there's only been one fatality (1963), and dorsal-fin sightings are rare enough to make the nightly news. Realistically, you're more likely to get hit by a bus, so get wet and enjoy yourself!

🚇 **Convention** 🚢 **Darling Harbour Aquarium**; ♿

Aqua-fans enter through huge, kitsch metallic shark jaws into 160m of underwater tunnels, looking at 11,000 happy Australian sea creatures. Highlights include clown fish, humungous sharks in the Open Ocean section and the Great Barrier Reef exhibit's swoon-worthy Van Gogh coral colours. Residents of the Seal Sanctuary have lawless amounts of fun. Arrive early to beat the crowds (but less chatter makes it harder to ignore the piped indigestive whale noises).

📷 SYDNEY WILDLIFE WORLD
☎ 9333 9288; www.sydneywildlife world.com.au; Aquarium Pier, Darling Harbour; admission $32/22.50, Wildlife Australia Pass incl admission to Sydney Wildlife World & Sydney Aquarium & return ferry from Circular Quay $55/28; ⏰ 9am-10pm, last admission 9pm; 🚇 Town Hall Ⓜ Darling Park 🚇 Convention 🚢 Darling Harbour Aquarium; ♿

The newest of Darling Harbour's attractions costs a pretty penny,

but it's a cut above the rest. And if you don't have time to truck out to Taronga Zoo, this is your chance to check out some Aussie critters! Nine different habitats with 1km of walkways give you a sense of how wild life really is for koalas, wallabies, birds, butterflies and reptiles (among others). Feedings and demonstrations happen throughout the day. Ask about combined admission prices to Wildlife World and the Sydney Aquarium next door.

 SHOP

📷 CYRIL'S FINE FOODS
Food & Drink
☎ 9211 0994; 181 Hay St, Haymarket; ⏰ 6am-5pm Mon-Fri, to 1pm Sat; 🚇 Central Ⓜ Powerhouse Museum 🚇 Capitol Square 🚌 George St buses

Cyril Vincent has opened his old-style deli at the crack of dawn for almost 50 years. Dawn doesn't seem to mind, and his loyal customers keep coming back for European smallgoods, chocolates, cheeses, coffee, mustards and variously pickled things at non-gourmet prices.

Paddy's Markets: an Aladdin's cave for bargain-hunters

☐ GOOD LIVING GROWERS' MARKET *Market*

☎ 9282 3606; www.events.smh.com.au;
Pyrmont Bay Park, Pyrmont; ⏰ 7-11am
1st Sat of each month; Ⓜ Harbourside
🚆 ⛴ Pyrmont Bay

This picturesque foodies' market
not far from Darling Harbour showcases the best New South Wales
(NSW) regional produce. Peruse
the 90 stalls packed with all sorts of
delicacies from goat's cheese and
sourdough bread to smoked tuna
and wattleseed ice cream. Grab
a coffee and reconstitute with an
egg, bacon and chutney roll.

☐ PADDY'S MARKETS *Market*

☎ 1300 361 589; www.paddysmarkets
.com.au; cnr Hay & Thomas Sts, Haymarket; ⏰ 9am-5pm Thu-Sun; 🚆 Central
Ⓜ Powerhouse Museum 🚆 Haymarket
🚌 George St buses

Paddy's is the Sydney equivalent
of Istanbul's Grand Bazaar, but
swap the incense, hookahs and
carpets for mobile-phone covers,
Eminem T-shirts and cheap sneak-
ers. There's more than 1000 stalls
in this cavernous space – pick up
a Victoria Bitter (VB) singlet for
Uncle Bruce or wander the aisles
in capitalist awe.

☐ ULTIMO WINE CENTRE
Food & Drink

☎ 9211 2380; www.ultimowinecentre
.com.au; 99 Jones St, Ultimo; ⏰ 9am-
7pm Mon-Wed, to 8pm Thu & Fri,
10am-8pm Sat, 12.30pm-4.30pm Sun;
🚃 🚃 Central 🚌 501

Sydney's leading wine import
specialist is just a cork's pop away
from Darling Harbour, with wines
divided regionally and special
sections devoted to books and
boozy accessories. Saturday-
afternoon wine tasting sessions
are timely.

EAT

🍴 BBQ KING *Cantonese* $$

☎ 9267 2586; fax 9267 2001; 18-20
Goulburn St, Chinatown; ⏰ 11.30am-
2am; 🚃 Central Ⓜ Garden Plaza
🚃 Capitol Square 🚌 George St buses;
🚻 Ⓥ

Low on ambience but big on
flavour, the King serves up royal
portions of roast duck, suckling
pig and other Cantonese staples.
You might need a Tsing Tao or
three to stay sane amid the mildly
obnoxious chaos. Take-away bald
glazed ducks available next door;
open late.

🍴 BLACKBIRD *Mod Oz* $$

☎ 9283 7385; www.blackbirdcafe.com
.au; Balcony, Cockle Bay Wharf, Darling
Harbour; ⏰ 8am-late; 🚃 Town Hall

Ⓜ Darling Park 🚃 Convention 🚃 Darling Harbour Aquarium; 🚹 🚹 Ⓥ
This place veritably thrums from
the minute it opens its doors for
breakfast. Funky young staff cruise
the cool interior delivering hearty
bowls of pasta, New York–style
pizzas from the hot-stone oven and
fat triangles of cake. Perfect to fuel
up before or after a big night out.

🍴 BUNGALOW 8 *Seafood* $$

☎ 9299 4660; www.bungalow8sydney
.com; 8 The Promenade, King St Wharf,
Darling Harbour; ⏰ noon-late;
🚃 Wynyard Ⓜ Darling Park
🚃 Harbourside 🚃 Darling Harbour
Aquarium; 🚹

Retreat to the far end of King St
Wharf if the mayhem of Darling
Harbour starts to melt your mind.
Slink into a low leather booth
on the cool slate floor, watch
the harbour lights and slurp a
lemongrass laksa stacked high
with fresh mussels. The Loft (p74)
bar upstairs has cool cocktails
afterwards.

**🍴 CHINATOWN NOODLE
RESTAURANT** *Cantonese* $

☎ 9281 9051; Shop 7, Prince Centre,
8 Quay St, Chinatown; ⏰ 11am-9pm;
🚃 Central Ⓜ Powerhouse Museum
🚃 Capitol Square 🚌 George St buses;
🚻 Ⓥ

It's sweaty, shoulder-to-shoulder
eating beneath wreaths of plastic

NEIGHBOURHOODS

CHINATOWN & DARLING HARBOUR

CHINESE WHISPERS

Chinese people first came to Australia in 1840 when convict transportation ceased and labouring jobs became available. Thousands more arrived during the 1850s gold rush, but immigration stalled when the notorious 'White Australia' policy was enacted in 1861. In the 1870s Sydney's Chinese community gravitated to Dixon St, which rapidly became a commercial centre tainted with opium dens and gambling. It's here that perhaps China's greatest gift to Australia still thrills the crowds – fabulous Chinese food!

grapes in this busy noodle nook, where the stringy fare is made fresh daily. The combination dish looks like spaghetti bolognaise on steroids – masses of thick wheat noodles, pork, shredded cucumber and lashings of chilli and black vinegar. Entry is from Thomas St.

🍴 CHINTA RIA, TEMPLE OF LOVE *Malaysian* $$

☎ 9264 3211; www.chintaria.com; L2, Cockle Bay Wharf, Darling Harbour; ⏱ noon-2.30pm Mon-Sat, 6-11pm daily; 🚊 Town Hall Ⓜ Darling Park 🚊 Convention Ⓜ Darling Harbour Aquarium; ♿ 🚶 Ⓥ

Swirling choreographically around an enormous concrete Buddha, Chinta Ria's temple-in-the-round offers zingy Malaysian hawker-

style food at reasonable prices. Go with a rabble of friends for Hokkien noodles, sambal prawns, seafood laksa, superslippery fried rice noodles and flaky roti bread.

🍴 GOLDEN CENTURY
Cantonese Seafood $$$

☎ 9212 3901; www.goldencentury .com.au; 393-399 Sussex St, Chinatown; ⏱ noon-4am; 🚊 Central Ⓜ Garden Plaza 🚊 Capitol Square 🚌 George St buses; ♿

The fish tank at this frenetic place forms a window-wall to the street, full of a whole lot o' nervous coral trout, king crab, barramundi, lobster and abalone. Splash out on the whole lobster cooked in ginger and shallots: tank–net– kitchen–you.

🍴 XIC LO *Vietnamese* $$

☎ 9280 1678; 215a Thomas St, Chinatown; ⏱ 11am-10.30pm Mon-Sat, to 10pm Sun; 🚊 Central Ⓜ Powerhouse Museum 🚊 Capitol Square 🚌 George St buses; 🚶 Ⓥ

Xic Lo's shiny, angular interior is a glossy departure from the daggy *pho* houses of yore. The menu though is reassuringly familiar: fresh rice-paper rolls, vermicelli salads and piping-hot bowls of aromatic *pho* soup (slippery rice noodles, fragrant basil and beef) are the stars. Enter from Ultimo Rd.

Feast on laksa, *pho* (Vietnamese noodle soup) and rice-paper rolls in bustling Chinatown

🍴 ZAAFFRAN *Indian* $$
☎ 9211 8900; www.zaaffran.com; L2, 345
Harbourside, Darling Harbour; 🕙 noon-
2.30pm daily, 6-9pm Sun-Thu, 6-10.15pm
Fri & Sat; 🚈 Town Hall Ⓜ 🚈 Convention
🚢 Pyrmont Bay; 🚻 Ⓥ
In a city with a gazillion cheap
Indian joints, this is a standout.
Authentic and innovative curries
are served up with awesome views
across Darling Harbour. Book a
balcony seat and launch into the
beef vindaloo.

🍸 DRINK
🍸 CARGO BAR *Bar*
☎ 9262 1777; www.cargobar.com
.au; 52 The Promenade, King St Wharf,
Darling Harbour; admission free;
🕙 11am-late; 🚈 Town Hall Ⓜ Darling
Park 🚢 Darling Harbour Aquarium; 🚻
The definitive Darling Harbour bar
lures beautiful boys, babes and
backpackers who get wall-to-wall
boozy after 11pm. It also has a
cool kitchen: before the drinkers

descend, savour the harbour views and tasty pizzas and salads. DJs fire things up nightly; Cargo Lounge upstairs is, well…loungier.

☑ THE LOFT *Bar*
☎ 9299 4770; www.theloftsydney.com; 3 Lime St, Darling Harbour; admission free; ⏱ 4pm-1am Mon-Wed, to 3am Thu, noon-3am Fri & Sat, noon-1am Sun; 🚆 Wynyard Ⓜ Darling Park 🚋 Harbourside 🚢 Darling Harbour Aquarium

The Loft is far from lofty – it's more like an open-plan office space – but the walls fold back and disappear, sweeping your eye out across Darling Harbour and beyond. Interior design is 'Moroccan Chic'; service is snappy. Book for high tea at high noon on weekends.

PLAY

☆ HOME *Club*
☎ 9266 0600; www.homesydney.com; Cockle Bay Wharf, Darling Harbour; admission free-$49; ⏱ bar 11am-late daily, club 9pm-late Thu-Sun; 🚆 Town Hall Ⓜ Darling Park 🚢 Darling Harbour Aquarium; ♿

Welcome to the pleasure dome: a three-level, 2000-capacity timber and glass 'prow' that's home to a huge dance floor, countless bars, outdoor balconies and sonics that make other clubs sound like transistor radios. Catch top-name international DJs spinning a

homey House smorgasbord, plus live bands amping it up.

☐ JAMES CRAIG
Organised Tour
☎ 9298 3888; www.sydneyheritage fleet.com.au; Wharf 7, Pyrmont; tickets $205/160; ⏱ 9.30am-4pm most weekends (Sat or Sun); Ⓜ Harbourside 🚋 🚢 Pyrmont Bay; ♿

The *James Craig* is a hulking, black, three-masted iron barque built in Sunderland, England in 1874. Abandoned in Tasmania in the '30s, she was floated to Sydney and restored in the '70s. Square-rigged sails billow as you sail out through the Heads on the open-ocean swell. Price includes lunch, morning/afternoon teas and a sea shanty or three.

☆ SLIP INN *Club*
☎ 8295 9999; www.merivale.com; 111 Sussex St; admission free-$25; ⏱ noon-1am Mon-Thu, noon-4am Fri, 6pm-4am Sat; 🚆 Wynyard Ⓜ Darling Park 🚢 Darling Harbour Aquarium; ♿

Slip into this warren of moody rooms on the edge of Darling Harbour and bump hips with the cool kids. Can you believe Crown Prince Frederik of Denmark met his Tasmanian missus here? Resident and international selectors serve up old-school funk, latin, breaks, tech and House. Refuel on pizza and Thai.

⭐ SYDNEY BY SAIL
Activity
☎ 9280 1110; www.sydneybysail.com
.au; Festival Pontoon, National Maritime
Museum, Darling Harbour; tour $150,
course $425; ☽ 9am-5pm; 🚊 Town Hall
Ⓜ Harbourside 🚊 🚢 Pyrmont Bay
Driving around driving you mad?
Sydney by Sail runs a daily sailing
tour and a comprehensive introductory weekend sailing course.
Knots, fathoms, hulls, bilges, spin-
nakers, tacking and gibing – 12
hours on the water will ensure
you're shipshape.

⭐ SYDNEY ENTERTAINMENT
CENTRE *Live Music*
☎ 9320 4200; www.sydentcent.com
.au; 35 Harbour St, Haymarket; ☽ box
office 9am-5pm Mon-Fri; 🚊 Central
Ⓜ Powerhouse Museum 🚊 Haymarket; ♿ 🚻
Sydney's largest indoor venue
holds 12,000 howling rock fans, recent acts including everyone from
Pink to Liza Minnelli, Alice Cooper
and the Dalai Lama (he rocks!). Its
padded purple seats also fill with
kids going nuts for the Wiggles
and Disney On Ice.

>INNER WEST

Paddington and the Eastern Beaches define Sydney at face value, but the Inner West digs deeper and comes up with something resembling a soul. This is where anyone with any sense of quirkiness hangs out – students, Goths, urban hippies, junkies, poets, painters, writers and sexual subculturists. Streets and shop windows have a decidedly less polished appearance around here – more graffiti, less Gucci.

Glebe focuses on Glebe Point Rd, a long, undulating strip of cafés, bookshops and eateries. The mood here is chilled-out, but the Saturday market (p78) injects some vigour – stock up on retro duds, jewellery, sunglasses and vinyl, and save space for a funky vego lunch. Newtown is much more hustle-and-bustle, the sinuous snake of King St is crammed tightly with restaurants, pubs, yoga studios and second-hand CD shops. This is also the spiritual home of Sydney's lesbian community. Further west are low-key Camperdown, rockin' Annandale, and leafy, affluent Balmain.

INNER WEST

🜃 SEE
Camperdown
    Cemetery 1 B5

🏠 SHOP
Berkelouw Books 2 C5
Deus Ex Machina 3 B4
Glebe Market 4 D3
Gleebooks 5 D3
Gleebooks
    (secondhand) 6 D3
Holy Moley 7 B6
Sydney Fish Market 8 D1

🍴 EAT
Badde Manors 9 D3
Boathouse on
    Blackwattle Bay 10 C1
Campos 11 C5
Corner Bar & Café 12 C6
Gallery Café 13 A3
Green Gourmet 14 C5
Kilimanjaro 15 C5
Old Fish Shop Café 16 B5
Spanish Tapas 17 D3
Thai Pothong 18 B5

🍸 DRINK
Courthouse Hotel 19 B5
Friend in Hand
    Hotel 20 D3

⭐ PLAY
Annandale Hotel 21 A4
Dendy Newtown 22 B5
Empire Hotel 23 A4
Enmore Theatre 24 A6
Sandringham Hotel 25 B6
Seymour Theatre
    Centre 26 D4
Vanguard 27 C5

SEE

CAMPERDOWN CEMETERY

☎ 9557 2043; www.ststephens.org.au;
187 Church St, Newtown; admission free;
🕐 6am-7pm; 🚉 Newtown 🚌 422-3,
426, 428; 🚻

Take a self-guided tour beyond
the monstrous 1848 fig tree
into this dark, eerily unkempt
cemetery. Many famous early Australians were buried here between
1849 and 1942, including Eliza
Donnithorne, the inspiration for
Miss Havisham in Dickens' *Great
Expectations*.

SHOP

DEUS EX MACHINA *Fashion*

☎ 9519 3983; www.deusexmachina
.com.au; 98-104 Parramatta Rd, Camperdown; 🕐 10am-6pm Mon-Fri, to 4pm
Sat; 🚌 423, 426, 440

Literally: 'God out of a machine',
this is the perfect example of how
big cities allow weird specialisa-
tions to flourish. Crammed with
classic and custom-made motor-
cycles, this is 'postmodern motor-
cyclism' at its best – part workshop,
part café, part offbeat boutique.

GLEBE MARKET *Market*

☎ 4237 7499; www.glebemarkets.com
.au; Glebe Public School, cnr Glebe Point
Rd & Derby Pl, Glebe; 🕐 9am-4pm Sat;
🚌 431-4

If you missed Woodstock, you'll
find its dreadlocked, shoeless
legacy here. Inner-city hippies
beat a hazy course to this crowded
Saturday market. Once mas-
saged, fuelled on lentil burgers
and swathed in funky retro gear,
they retreat to the lawns, pass
the peace pipe and chill-out to an
African drum soundtrack.

GLEEBOOKS *Bookshop*

☎ 9660 2333; www.gleebooks.com.au;
49 Glebe Point Rd, Glebe; 🕐 9am-9pm;
🚌 431-4

Gleebooks – a ramshackle two-
storey terrace house – is generally
regarded as Sydney's best bookshop. The aisles are packed with
politics, arts and general fiction and

WORTH THE TRIP

Milling around the shady grounds of St Andrews Congregational, **Balmain Market**
(☎ 0418-765 736; www.balmainmarket.com.au; cnr Darling St & Curtis Rd, Balmain;
🕐 8.30am-4pm Sat; 🚢 Balmain East 🚌 432-4, 441-2, 445) features stalls selling arts,
crafts, books, clothing, jewellery, plants and fruit and veg, all jumbled together like socks
in a drawer. The church itself is open if you want a Middle Eastern snack or need to consult
St Andy about a prospective purchase.

staff know their stuff backwards. Its annual literary programme attracts big-name local (Winton, Leunig etc) and international writers. Children's and second-hand books are at the second branch at 191 Glebe Point Rd.

HOLY MOLEY *Fashion*
☎ 9550 4033; www.holymoley
.moonfruit.com; 325 King St, Newtown;
⏰ 11am-5pm Sun-Wed, to 8pm Thu, to
6pm Fri & Sat; ⓡ Newtown

You can't miss Holy Moley's murals of Bob DeNiro in *Taxi Driver* and an

Get your motor runnin' at Deus ex Machina

Thumb through the volumes at Sydney's much-loved Gleebooks (p78)

axe-wielding Jack Nicholson in *The Shining*. Inside it's all spunky-punky T-shirts, studded belts, baby-doll dresses and sexy lingerie. 'Don't be shy!' say the girl staff, modelling the merchandise for each other, 'You can come in – we're dressed now.'

SYDNEY FISH MARKET
Food & Drink

☎ 9004 1100; www.sydneyfishmarket .com.au; Bank St, Pyrmont; ⏰ 7am-4pm; 🚊 Fish Market 🚌 501, 443

This piscatorial precinct on Blackwattle Bay has restaurants, a deli, wine centre, oyster bar, florist, seafood school, early morning auctions and behind-the-scenes auction tours ($20; 6.55am Monday and Thursday). Chefs, locals and overfed seagulls haggle over oysters, mud crabs, Balmain bugs, lobsters and slabs of salmon.

EAT

BADDE MANORS
Café $

☎ 9660 3797; www.baddemanorscafe .com; 37 Glebe Point Rd, Glebe; ⏰ 8am-midnight Mon-Thu, to 1am Fri & Sat, 9am-midnight Sun; 🚌 431-4; ♿ Ⓥ
The feeling's eclectically old-world, but Badde Manors is a new-age kinda joint. It can get hectic here, but service remains cool and composed – no sign of the alleged bad manners. Dogs sleep blissfully outside, dreaming of the Portuguese custard tarts and rhubarb crumble behind the glass.

BOATHOUSE ON BLACKWATTLE BAY
Seafood $$$

☎ 9518 9011; www.boathouse.net.au; end of Ferry Rd, Glebe; ⏰ noon-3pm & 6-10pm Tue-Sun; 🚆 Glebe 🚌 431-4
The best restaurant in Glebe, and one of the best seafood restaurants in Sydney. Offerings range

from oysters so fresh you'd think you shucked them yourself, to a snapper pie that'll go straight to the top of your favourite dish list. Anzac Bridge views; reservations essential.

CAMPOS
Café $

☎ 9516 3361; www.camposcoffee .com; 193 Missenden Rd, Newtown; ⏰ 7am-4pm Mon-Fri, 8am-5pm Sat; 🚆 Newtown 🚌 422-3, 426, 428; ♿
Trying to squeeze into crowded Campos, king of Sydney's bean-scene, can be a challenge. Caffeine fiends come from miles around – hat-wearing students, broadsheet literati, window-seat daydreamers and doctors on a break from the hospital – all gagging for a shot of 'Campos Superior' blend. The closest competition is in northern Italy.

CORNER BAR & CAFÉ
Wine Bar & Café $$

☎ 9519 9911; 93 Erskineville Rd, Erskineville; ⏰ 7am-11pm Tue-Thu, to midnight Fri, 8am-late Sat & Sun; 🚆 Erskineville
In emerging Erskineville village, this breezy street-corner wine bar does a brisk breakfast trade, moving on to pizzas and tapas later in the day. Order a few plates and a glass of vino and hit the footpath tables.

Sophie Du Bois
Sydney fashion designer (www.sophiedubois.net)

Is there a Sydney 'look'? Bondi is cutting-edge and expressive; Double Bay is 'designer'; Newtown is street, vintage and punk…but really, anything goes here! The vibe is beachy and summery: lots of skin, lots of short dresses. **Favourite Sydney designers?** Sass & Bide (p117) is *very* Sydney: short, tight and sexy. Belinda's Corner Shop (p113) has amazing labels. For guys I like Calibre (p114) and Herringbone (p115). Big names like Collette Dinnigan (p114) are brilliant, but they're expensive if you're buying a piece every week! **Sydney's best shopping?** Sydney's weekend markets: Bondi (p123), Paddington (p116), Glebe (p78). Newtown for little side-street boutiques, Queen St, Woollahra (p116) for designer gear; and Crown St, Surry Hills (p91) for vintage stuff. **Where is Sydney on the world fashion stage?** We've definitely got an edgy, climate-driven style, using more natural fibres than synthetics. We're moving into a 'greener' age – Sydneysiders wear clothing that reflects this lifestyle.

WORTH THE TRIP
The culinary highlight of Leichhardt, Sydney's Italian district just west of Annandale, is **Grappa** (☎ 9560 6090; www.grappa.com.au; Shop 1, 267-277 Norton St, Leichhardt; 🕐 6-10pm Mon, noon-3pm & 6-10pm Tue-Fri, 6-11pm Sat, noon-3pm & 6-9.30pm Sun; 🚌 413, 435-8, 440; ♿). An open kitchen, snazzy bar and cream-leather seats provide the setting for rich, succulent dishes (such as baked snapper in rock-salt crust) and bounteous wood-fired pizzas. If it's warm, sit outside on the terrace, sip chianti and think of Tuscany. *Ahhh*, Tuscany…

🍴 GALLERY CAFÉ
Café $
☎ 9692 8449; www.gallerycafe.com.au; 43 Booth St, Annandale; 🕐 7am-5.30pm Mon-Sat, 8am-5pm Sun; 🚌 470; ♿
The barista here has the coolest full-sleeve tattoo ever. We can't guarantee he'll make your coffee, but order a New York–style turkey and cranberry toasted sandwich (heavy on the bird) regardless, and check out the art-hung walls.

🍴 GREEN GOURMET
Vegetarian $
☎ 9519 5330; www.greengourmet.com.au; 115 King St, Newtown; 🕐 noon-3pm & 6-10pm; 🚊 Newtown 🚌 422-3, 426, 428; V
Green Gourmet is a self-serve, pay-per-kilo, kind-to-animals eatery, plating up Chinese-Malaysian vegetarian at affordable prices. On weekends, grab a few morsels of cruelty-free yum cha and wash it down with one of the excellent teas on offer. Alcohol-free too.

🍴 KILIMANJARO *African* $$
☎ 9557 4565; fax 9565 1869; 280 King St, Newtown; 🕐 noon-3pm & 6-10pm Sun-Thu, 6-11pm Fri & Sat; 🚊 Newtown 🚌 422-3, 426, 428; V
The cosy tables, carved-wooden bowls, saffron aromas and cheery atmosphere will raise your appetite high above the Serengeti. Authentic East African dishes such as the *yassa* (chicken on the bone marinated in spicy tomato sauce) are utterly filling. Check out the crafty Africa mural on the alleyway wall!

🍴 OLD FISH SHOP CAFÉ
Café $
☎ 9519 4295; fax 9565 1532; 239a King St, Newtown; 🕐 6am-7pm; 🚊 Newtown 🚌 422-3, 426, 428; ♿ V
In a converted fish shop (no prizes for figuring that out), this is Newtown's tattooed, dreadlocked, caffeine-hungry hub. Friendly pierced staff will fix you a double shot as you put your feet up on the cushions in the window and watch the freak-show on the street.

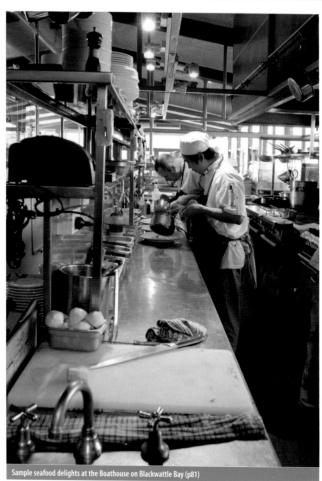

Sample seafood delights at the Boathouse on Blackwattle Bay (p81)

SPANISH TAPAS
Spanish $$

☎ 9571 9005; www.spanishtapas
.com.au; 26 Glebe Point Rd, Glebe;
noon-3pm Thu-Sat, 6-11pm daily;
431-4; V

This is a good-time restaurant: shared tapas plates, spirited music, raucous diners and waiters who say, 'Yezz, we jave a table forl yo'. Cheap jugs of sangria will dissolve any party resistance and fire you up for flamenco dancing displays.

THAI POTHONG *Thai* $$

☎ 9550 6277; www.thaipothong.com.au; 294 King St, Newtown; noon-3pm Tue-Sun, 6-10pm Sun-Thu, 6-11pm Fri & Sat; Newtown 422-3, 426, 428; V

This place has won a bowlful of 'Best Thai Restaurant in Sydney' awards. The menu is predictable and the usual rabble of golden Buddhas festoons the walls, but the mood is oddly romantic. Pull up a window seat and watch the Newtowners pass onwards to oblivion.

DRINK

COURTHOUSE HOTEL *Pub*

☎ 9519 8273; 202 Australia St, Newtown; 10am-midnight Mon-Sat, to 10pm Sun; Newtown

What a brilliant pub! The 150-year-old Courthouse is the kind

WORTH THE TRIP
The Harbour Bridge views from the long balcony at Balmain's **London Hotel** (☎ 9555 1377; www.thelondonhotel.com.au; 234 Darling St, Balmain; admission free; 11am-midnight Mon-Sat, noon-10pm Sun; Balmain East 432-4, 441-2, 445) are quintessentially Sydney (about as far from London as you can get). There's a great range of Oz beers on tap, plus a few quality Euro interlopers (Heineken, Hoegaarden et al), jovial punters and nonstop rugby on the telly.

of place where everyone from pool-playing Goth lesbians to magistrates can have a beer and feel right at home. Drink specials, decent house red and good pub grub too.

FRIEND IN HAND HOTEL
Pub

☎ 9660 2326; www.friendinhand.com.au; 58 Cowper St, Glebe; admission free; 10am-late; 431-4;

This place has changed the rules of what's supposed to happen in an Australian pub. Sure, you can drink all the beer you want, but don't be surprised when the eating competitions, water-pistol fights, crab racing, stand-up comedians, cheesy Joel/John piano men and hula-hoop spin-offs cut into your drinking time.

PLAY

⭐ ANNANDALE HOTEL
Live Music

☎ 9550 1078; www.annandalehotel
.com; cnr Parramatta Rd & Nelson St, Annandale; admission free-$30; ⌚ 5-10pm
Mon & Tue, to midnight Wed, noon-1am
Thu-Sat, noon-midnight Sun; 🚆 Stanmore 🚌 413, 435-8, 440, 461; 🚻

The Annandale survived Sydney's
live-music morgue in the '90s and
now spearheads Sydney's rock
revival, coughing up nightly alt-
rock, metal, punk and electronica.
Afroed punters traverse the sticky
carpet between sets by Thirsty
Merc, the Dandy Warhols and
Jet. 'F*£k this, I'm going to the
Annandale!'

⭐ EMPIRE HOTEL
Live Music

☎ 9557 1701; www.empirelive.com
.au; cnr Parramatta Rd & Johnston St, Annandale; admission free-$20; ⌚ 10am-
midnight Mon & Tue, to 3am Wed-Sat, to
10pm Sun; 🚆 Stanmore 🚌 413, 435-8,
440, 461; 🚻

The Empire's well-managed
300-capacity bar gets down 'n'
dirty with some of Sydney's best
blues and roots. Local bands with
loyal followings play free gigs;
listen out for international artists
and regular metal, ska, rockabilly,
country-and-western and swing
dancing nights!

WORTH THE TRIP

The well-restored late-Victorian **Dawn
Fraser Baths** (☎ 9555 1903; www
.leichhardt.nsw.gov.au/dfb.html; El-
kington Park, Glassop St, Balmain;
admission $3.80/$2.60; ⌚ 7.15am-
5.30pm Mar-Nov, 6.45am-7pm Dec-
Feb; 🚌 432-4, 441-2, 445) are worth
a look. Built in 1884, the enclosure
protects swimmers from underwater
undesirables. Australia's all-conquering
1956–64 Olympian Dawn Fraser spent
far too long swimming laps here.

⭐ ENMORE THEATRE
Live Music

☎ 9550 3666; www.enmoretheatre
.com.au; 130 Enmore Rd, Newtown;
tickets $20-60; ⌚ box office 9am-6pm
Mon-Fri, 10am-4pm Sat; 🚆 Newtown
🚌 422-3, 426, 428; 🚻 🚻

Originally a vaudeville playhouse,
the elegantly wasted Enmore
now hosts acts like Queens of the
Stone Age, Wilco and PJ Harvey,
plus theatre and comedy. The
1600-capacity theatre feels like
an old-time movie hall, with café,
wooden floors, lounge areas and
balconies.

⭐ SANDRINGHAM HOTEL
Live Music

☎ 9557 1254; www.sando.com.au; 387
King St, Newtown; admission free-$15;
⌚ 9.30am-midnight Mon-Wed, to 2am
Thu & Fri, 10am-2am Sat, 10am-10pm

Sun; 🚇 Newtown 🚌 422-3, 426, 428
We were rather nervous the Sando's renovations would spell the end of live music here, but thankfully, you can still get rocked-out from Tuesday to Sunday for not much money. Acoustic acts upstairs; Goth-metal on Sunday night.

⭐ **SEYMOUR THEATRE CENTRE** *Theatre*
☎ 9351 7940; www.seymourcentre .com.au; cnr City Rd & Cleveland St, Newtown; tickets from $25; 🕐 box office 9am-6pm Mon-Fri, 11am-3pm Sat; 🚌 422-3
Behind a glass curtain-wall on an insanely busy intersection, this Sydney University–affiliated theatre (actually, four theatres) shows an eclectic selection of plays, cabaret, comedy and musicals. Thirsty? There's a bar here too. Peckish? The centre fires up a 'gourmet bbq' in the front courtyard.

⭐ **VANGUARD** *Live Music*
☎ 9557 7992; www.thevanguard.com .au; 42 King St, Newtown; dinner & show per person from $40, general admission $10-40; 🕐 6.30pm-midnight Tue-Sun; 🚇 Newtown; 🚌 422-3, 426, 428
Freethinking, intellectual, artistic, musical – the qualities to which the Vanguard aspires. The intimate, time-travelling 1920s-themed band room satisfies these criteria; occasional Russell Crowe gigs, however, do not. Jeff Martin and Holly Throsby shows are redemptive. Most seats are reserved for dinner-and-show diners.

>SURRY HILLS

Jammed between Darlinghurst and the city, Surry Hills is home to a raffish, noir mishmash of inner-city groovers and yuppies, many of whom rarely venture beyond their favourite (and admittedly excellent) local pubs and eateries. Fed and watered, they drift back to their slick warehouse apartments, remnants of the rag trade and print industry upon which Surry Hills built its reputation. But don't expect much gritty blue-collar struggle around here – life for 'Surry Hillbillies' these days is decadent, comfortable and sophisticated.

Most of the Surry Hills action centres on Crown St and Bourke St, heading south from the city – both streets have clusters of excellent restaurants, cafés and pubs. Surry Hills also sustains a collection of cutting-edge and crafty galleries (including the converted studio of legendary Surry Hills local Brett Whiteley), actively engaging in artsy sabre-rattling with the snootier rival galleries in Paddington, and the hip new galleries along Danks St in Waterloo.

SURRY HILLS

SEE
Brett Whiteley Studio	...1	C5
Object Gallery	...2	D3
Ray Hughes Gallery	...3	C5

SHOP
Orson & Blake	...4	B5
Spence & Lyda	...5	B2
Sydney Antique Centre	...6	D5

EAT
bills Surry Hills	...7	C3
Billy Kwong	...8	C3
Bird Cow Fish	...9	C5
Bodega	...10	B3
Book Kitchen	...11	C5
Bourke St Bakery	...12	C5
Longrain	...13	B2
Marque	...14	C3
Pizza e Birra	...15	C5
Tabou	...16	C5

DRINK
Cricketers Arms Hotel	...17	D4
Hotel Hollywood	...18	B2
Mars Lounge	...19	B1

PLAY
Company B	...20	B5
Gaelic Club	...21	A4
Hopetoun Hotel	...22	D4

NEIGHBOURHOODS

SURRY HILLS

SEE

BRETT WHITELEY STUDIO
☎ 9225 1881; www.brettwhiteley.org;
2 Raper St; admission free; ⏰ 10am-
4pm Sat & Sun; 🚉 🚋 Central 🚌 301-3,
343, 372
Whiteley was rock 'n' roll artistry –
he lived fast and without restraint,
and when he let fly on the canvas,

everybody went 'Ooohh!' His
studio has been preserved as a
gallery for some of his best work.
Get in early for weekend discus-
sions, performances, readings and
workshops.

OBJECT GALLERY
☎ 9361 4555; www.object.com.au; 415
Bourke St; admission free; ⏰ 11am-6pm

Brett Whiteley's most intriguing works are preserved in this studio-turned-gallery

Tue-Sun; 🚇 Central 🚌 371, 373, 377, 380, 396; ♿
Inside the former St Margaret's Hospital chapel (a 1958 modernist classic by architect Ken Woolley), nonprofit Object presents innovative exhibitions of new craft and design from Australia and overseas. Furniture, fashion, textiles and glass festoon three levels.

🎨 RAY HUGHES GALLERY
☎ 9698 3200; www.rayhughesgallery.com; 270 Devonshire St; admission free; 🕑 10am-6pm Tue-Sat; 🚆 🚇 Central 🚌 301
Beyond the corrugated-iron cows and enormous wooden fish, old-time art dealer Ray Hughes wheels and deals. The Australian and contemporary Chinese and African art he flogs is some of Sydney's classiest. His bohemian warehouse is worth a look.

SHOP
🏠 SPENCE & LYDA *Homewares*
☎ 9212 6747; www.spenceandlyda.com.au; 16 Foster St; 🕑 9am-5pm Mon-Fri, 10am-4pm Sat, 11am-4pm Sun ; 🚆 🚇 Central Ⓜ World Square 🚌 308-10, 343
Solid but far from rustic, bright but never garish, the Italian and US kitchenware, fabrics, furnishings, lamps, linen, glassware and rugs in this snazzy showroom will make

even the most determined travellers want to go home and feather the nest. Don't be deterred by the stern, deskbound staff – though we suspect they're bored, they are delighted to help.

🏺 SYDNEY ANTIQUE CENTRE
Antiques
☎ 9361 3244; www.sydantcent.com.au; 531 South Dowling St; 🕑 10am-6pm; 🚌 339, 340, 373-4, 390
Sydney's oldest antique shop, the capacious Sydney Antique Centre has more than 60 dealers specialising in porcelain, silver, glass, collectables and furniture. Items range from sports memorabilia to antique grandfather clocks and Art Deco jewellery. Pick up a 19th-century alabaster mannequin and drag it through the café and bookshop.

EAT
🍴 BILLY KWONG *Chinese* $$
☎ 9332 3300; www.kyliekwong.org/billykwongs.aspx; 3/355 Crown St; 🕑 6-10pm Mon-Sat, to 9pm Sun; 🚆 🚇 Central 🚌 301-3, 391; ♿ Ⓥ
Chef Kylie Kwong's novel take on Chinese cuisine soon explains why this hip eating house is always so busy. You can't go wrong with staples like spicy, diced, fried green beans with *hoisin* (sweet red sauce) and garlic, or a generous serve of Kylie's signature dish, the crispy-skin duck with plum sauce.

¶ BIRD COW FISH
Bistro & Deli $$

☎ 9380 4090; www.birdcowfish.com.au; 500 Crown St; ⏰ 11am-10pm Mon-Fri, 8am-10pm Sat, 8am-4pm Sun; 🚌 301-3, 391; ♿

As the name suggests, there's plenty of creatively prepared flesh on BCF's menu, but locals and cross-town venturers are here as much for the munificent *fromage* as the meat. Forty boutique Oz and in-ternational cheeses generate quite a whiff in the corner deli. Oh, and the espresso's as good as it gets!

¶ BODEGA *Spanish* $$

☎ 9212 7766; www.bodegatapas.com; 216 Commonwealth St, Surry Hills; ⏰ noon-3pm Thu & Fri, 6-10pm Mon-Sat; 🚆 Central

Sydney's coolest tapas bar, casual Bodega has good-lookin' staff and a funky matador mural. Dishes range from spiced pumpkin and feta empanadas to hefty slabs of seared salmon with tahini and pickled cucumber. Wash 'em down with Hispanic wine and plenty of Mediterranean gusto.

¶ BOOK KITCHEN *Café* $$

☎ 9310 1003; www.thebookkitchen.com.au; 255 Devonshire St; ⏰ 8am-4pm daily, 6.30-10.30pm Thu-Sat; 🚌 301-3, 391; ♿ Ⓥ

Sunny footpath tables, attentive service, walls of foody books, a braised Wagyu beef and mustard sandwich and a Book Kitchen Bloody Mary – sometimes life just comes together perfectly doesn't it?

¶ BOURKE ST BAKERY *Café* $

☎ 9699 1011; 633 Bourke St; ⏰ 7am-7pm Tue-Fri, 8am-5pm Sat & Sun; 🚌 301-3, 391; ♿ ♿ Ⓥ

It has been around a scant few years but the Bourke St Bakery has quickly become an essential Surry Hills experience, offering up a mean selection of pastries, cakes, croissants, tarts, quiches and organic breads, all baked with that rare combo of deliciousness, dedication and delight. If you're hung-over, the coffee will right your rudder.

¶ LONGRAIN *Thai* $$$

☎ 9280 2888; www.longrain.com.au; 85 Commonwealth St; ⏰ noon-2.30pm Mon-Fri, 6-11pm Mon-Sat, bar 5.30pm-midnight Mon-Sat; 🚆 🚆 Central Ⓜ World Square 🚌 308-10, 343; ♿ Ⓥ

Longrain makes serving dozens of louche diners look easy. Inside a century-old, wedge-shaped printing-press building, urbanites slurp down delicacies such as red venison and snakebean curry or caramelised pork hock with five spices and chilli vinegar. Sip a caipiroska at the bar afterwards.

NEIGHBOURHOODS

SURRY HILLS

Andrew P Street
Sydney music journalist

Is there a 'Sydney Sound'? No, but different kinds of bands gravitate to certain venues: rock bands play at the Annandale Hotel (p86), indie-pop at the Hopetoun Hotel (p95), dance-punk at Spectrum (p107). **Is there more live music here now than five years ago?** Yeah, because the licensing laws have changed – it's cheaper and easier for pubs to do it now. **Fave venues?** Definitely the Metro (p46) – good sight-lines and a great PA. There's nothing like a full house at the Annandale, and the Hopetoun when it's not too packed. **Dance clubs?** Chinese Laundry at the Slip Inn (p74) has always done well. Home (p74) is still Sydney's big 'superclub'. **Best festivals?** All Tomorrow's Parties (p20) on Cockatoo Island was amazing this year. Homebake (p22) is a great celebration of Australian music, and the Mardi Gras (p20) is just insane of course.

NEIGHBOURHOODS

SURRY HILLS

MARQUE French $$$

☎ 9332 2225; www.marquerestaurant
.com.au; 355 Crown St; ⏱ noon-2.30pm
Fri, 6.30-10pm Mon-Sat; 🚌 🚋 Central
🚌 301-3, 391; 👤

Marque's crisp, immaculate décor
provides a level-headed platform
for adventurous cooking. It's one
of those places where culinary
experimentation at first seems
ridiculous, but you walk away
smiling. Try the milk-fed veal
loin with Meyer lemon, liquorice,
pumpkin and coffee.

PIZZA E BIRRA Italian $$

☎ 9332 2510; 1/500 Crown St; ⏱ 6-
11pm Mon-Wed, noon-11pm Thu-Sun;
🚌 301-3, 391; 👤 👶 Ⓥ

Bentwood chairs clatter across
the polished concrete floor;
friends laugh, clink glasses and
unwind; waiters spin, smile and
style – Pizza e Birra is the perfect
neighbourhood bistro, with
enough style to be cool, and
enough familiarity to be comfortable. Try the classic Napoletana
pizza: tomato, mozzarella, olives
and anchovies, washed down
with a cold Peroni.

TABOU French $$$

☎ 9319 5682; www.tabourestaurant
.com.au; 527 Crown St; ⏱ 6.30pm-late
daily, noon-2.30pm Mon-Fri; 🚌 301-3, 391

Tabou's stained-glass shopfront
and lilting accordion music are

French to the core and it wouldn't
be out of place on Boulevard Saint-
Michel. Brasserie dishes, including
perennial faves such as duck confit,
lapin de la moutard (rabbit with
mustard sauce) and steak tartare,
paint the scene Gallic. *Vive la France*!

DRINK

CRICKETERS ARMS HOTEL
Pub

☎ 9331 3301; www.myspace.com/crick
etersarmshotel; 106 Fitzroy St; admission
free; ⏱ noon-midnight Mon-Sat, to
10pm Sun; 🚌 🚋 Central 🚌 374

The polysexual cricketers, with
its cruisy, cosy vibe, is a favourite
haunt of arts students, locals, gays
and turntable fans. It's ace for a
beer anytime, and there's tapas on
tap and open fires for those rare
times Sydney actually gets cold.

HOTEL HOLLYWOOD *Pub*

☎ 9281 2765; www.hotelhollywood
.com.au; 2 Foster St; admission free-$5;
⏱ 11am-midnight Mon-Wed, to 3am
Thu-Sat; 🚌 🚋 Central Ⓜ World
Square 🚌 308-10, 343

An inner-city, prow-shaped, Art
Deco gem, the Hollywood hasn't
felt the need to buff itself up to a
superficial sheen. A mixed (dare
we say, bohemian) crowd of Surry
Hillbillies gets down to serious
beer business. Live jazz Monday to
Wednesday from 8pm.

OUT ON THE TILES

Most of Sydney's older pubs are clad in glazed tiles, often with beautifully coloured Art Nouveau designs. Why? Prior to drinking law reform in the mid-1950s, pubs shut their doors at 6pm, before which after-work drinkers would storm in and chug down as many beers as quickly as possible – the 'six o'clock swill'. This, plus the sudden requirement of walking, caused frequent regurgitations, the nearest wall becoming a prop for the trembling vomiter. Publicans discovered pretty quickly that glazed tiles are easy to hose down.

🍸 MARS LOUNGE *Bar*
☎ 9267 6440; www.marslounge.com.au; 16 Wentworth Ave; admission free; ⏱ 5pm-midnight Wed, to 3am Fri, 7pm-3am Sat, 7pm-1am Sun; 🚇 Museum Ⓜ World Square 🚌 308-10, 343

Red leather booths; disco-ball reflections catching in the corner of your eye – Mars is *sooo* money. Sip a cocktail and try to stay focussed as you watch the bar staff in action, most of whom seem to be auditioning for a gig in a Justin Timberlake video.

⭐ PLAY
⭐ COMPANY B *Theatre*
☎ 9699 3444; www.belvoir.com.au; Belvoir Street Theatre, 25 Belvoir St; tickets from $56/34; ⏱ box office 9.30am-6pm Mon & Tue, to 7.30pm Wed-Sat, 2.30-7.30pm Sun; 🚇 🚌 Central; ♿

Artistic director Neil Armfield is the darling of the Sydney theatre world. Cinema stars such as Geoffrey Rush clamour to perform his interpretations of modern masters including David Hare in the recently refurbished Belvoir St Theatre. Book.

⭐ GAELIC CLUB
Live Music
☎ 9211 1687; www.thegaelicclub.com.au; 64 Devonshire St; tickets $10-30; 🚇 🚌 Central 🚌 Railway Sq buses

Rock into the Gaelic Club and get your earwax blasted out courtesy of select internationals such as Anti-Flag and Pony Up, or home-grown sonic assailants including Daysend, Gyroscope and Katalyst. It's a mid-size, split-level, multipurpose affair – much beer and moshing.

⭐ HOPETOUN HOTEL
Live Music
☎ 9361 5257; www.myspace.com/hopetounhotel; 416 Bourke St; admission free-$15; ⏱ 3pm-midnight Mon-Sat, 3-10pm Sun; 🚇 🚌 Central 🚌 374

Once the uncontested crucible for new Sydney rock bands, the diminutive 'Hoey' is still a launch pad for garage bands on the boil. On Sunday afternoon it transforms into a low-key space with DJs and night-crawlers knocking the froth off a few cold ones before they hit the sack.

>KINGS CROSS, DARLINGHURST & AROUND

Everything you've heard about Kings Cross is probably true – it retains a sleazy, cannibalistic aura – but the vague sense of menace is more imaginary than real. Sometimes the razzle-dazzle has a sideshow appeal; sometimes walking up Darlinghurst Rd promotes pity. Either way, it's never boring.

Darlinghurst is less clichéd in its debauchery, but many Darlinghursters are still the masters of their own nihilistic, pill-popping universe. Excellent coffee shops, pubs, bars and eateries line Darlinghurst Rd and Victoria St. The section of Oxford St running through Darlinghurst contains Sydney's best-known gay clubs.

KINGS CROSS, DARLINGHURST & AROUND

⊙ SEE
Aboriginal Fine Art Prints	1	B6
Artery	2	D5
Artspace	3	D2
Elizabeth Bay House	4	F2
Sydney Jewish Museum	5	D6

🛍 SHOP
Bookshop Darlinghurst	6	C7
Capital L	7	C8
C's Flashback	8	B7
Sedition	9	D6
Wheels & Doll Baby	10	B7

🍴 EAT
A Tavola	11	D6
Aki's	12	D2
Bar Coluzzi	13	D5

bills	14	D6
DOV at Delectica	15	C6
Fish Face	16	D6
Fratelli Paradiso	17	E2
Harry's Café de Wheels	18	D2
Hugo's Bar Pizza	(see 26)	
Libertine	19	E4
Otto	20	D2
Yellow	21	E2
Zinc	22	E2

🍸 DRINK
Darlo Bar	23	D6
Gazebo Wine Garden	24	F4
Green Park Hotel	25	D6
Hugo's Lounge	26	E5
Jimmy Lik's	27	D4
Old Fitzroy Hotel	28	D4
Oxford Hotel	29	B7
Ruby Rabbit	30	C7

Tilbury Hotel	31	D2
Victoria Room	32	D6
Water Bar	33	D2

⭐ PLAY
Arq	34	C7
Bar Me & El Rocco Jazz Cellar	35	D5
Candy's Apartment	36	E5
Darlinghurst Theatre Company	37	F3
Exchange Hotel	38	A6
Midnight Shift	39	B6
Slide	40	A6
Stables Theatre	41	D5
Stonewall Hotel	42	B7
Sydney by Diva	(see 29)	
Tonic Lounge	43	E4
Yu	44	D4

Please see over for map

In between Kings Cross and the harbour is Woolloomooloo (show us another word with eight 'o's!). The redevelopment of the wharf here has been a huge success, changing the formerly seedy enclave full of drunks, sailors and drunk sailors to a civilised, gourmet nook. Nearby, Potts Point and Elizabeth Bay are dignified, harbourside suburbs. See p13 for more.

SEE

ABORIGINAL FINE ART PRINTS

☎ 9332 1722; www.aboriginalartprints
.com.au; 68 Oxford St, Darlinghurst;
admission free; ☺ 9am-6pm Mon-Fri,
11am-6pm Sat, by appointment Sun;
🚇 Museum 🚌 378, 380, L82

Lustrous screen prints, rare limited editions, and quality lithographs, etchings and linocuts make this gallery a standout. It houses Sydney's most expansive collection by Australia's leading indigenous artists; look for works by Dennis Nona, Rover Thomas and Rosella Namok.

ARTERY

☎ 9380 8234; www.artery.com.au;
Shop 2, 221 Darlinghurst Rd, Darlinghurst; admission free; ☺ 10am-6pm
Mon-Sat; 🚇 Kings Cross 🚌 323-7,
324-5, 333, 389

More art retail than art gallery, this indigenous-art outlet deliberately steers away from the glitzy gallery scene, sourcing its contemporary, original selections from up-and-coming Central Australian artists. Prices are realistic and affordable; modern indigenous jewellery,

hand-woven baskets and gorgeous canvasses start around $30.

ARTSPACE

☎ 9368 1899; www.artspace.org.au;
The Gunnery, 43-51 Cowper Wharf
Rd, Woolloomooloo; admission free;
☺ 11am-5pm Tue-Sun; 🚌 311; 🚻
Artspace is spacey; the eternal quest is to fill the void with vigorous, engaging Australian and international contemporary art. Things here are decidedly avant-garde – expect lots of conceptual pieces, a-v installations and new-media masterpieces.

ELIZABETH BAY HOUSE

☎ 9356 3022; www.hht.net.au; 7
Onslow Ave, Elizabeth Bay; admission
$8/4; ☺ 9.30am-4pm Fri-Sun; 🚇 Kings
Cross 🚌 311

Built between 1835 and 1839 for Colonial Secretary Alexander Macleay, this elegant neoclassical mansion was the finest house in the colony. Ugly 20th-century apartments now surround it, but the exquisite oval salon and stairwell are timeless architectural delights. Wheelchair access to ground floor only.

KINGS CROSS, DARLINGHURST & AROUND

SYDNEY JEWISH MUSEUM

☎ 9360 7999; www.sydneyjewish museum.com.au; 148 Darlinghurst Rd, Darlinghurst; admission $10/7; ⏱ 10am-4pm Sun-Thu, to 2pm Fri, closed Jewish holidays; 🚇 Kings Cross 🚌 311, 389; ♿ Created as a living memorial to the Holocaust, the Sydney Jewish Museum examines Australian Jewish history, culture and tradition from the time of the First Fleet to the present day.

SHOP

BOOKSHOP
DARLINGHURST *Bookshop*

☎ 9331 1103; www.thebookshop .com.au; 207 Oxford St, Darlinghurst; ⏱ 10am-10pm Mon-Wed, to 11pm Thu, to midnight Fri & Sat, 11am-11pm Sun; 🚌 378, 380, 389
The obvious name doesn't inspire, but this large, fastidious gay and lesbian bookshop on the Oxford St 'Golden Mile' is far from lacklustre. Titles range from queer theory through to erotica, magazines and Australian fiction.

CAPITAL L *Fashion*

☎ 9361 0111; www.capital-l.com; 333 South Dowling St, Darlinghurst; ⏱ noon-6pm Mon-Wed, 11am-8pm Thu, 11am-6pm Fri & Sat, noon-5pm Sun; 🚌 378, 380, 389
Owner Louise stocks 52 funky up-and-coming designers to

complement those already in the limelight. Hip sales staff break from tradition and actually help you find and try on clothes by emerging local talents like Michelle Robinson.

C'S FLASHBACK *Fashion*

☎ 9331 7833; 316 Crown St, Darlinghurst; ⏱ 10am-6pm Mon-Wed, Fri & Sat, to 9pm Thu, 11am-5.30pm Sun; 🚌 380
Looking for a second-hand Hawaiian shirt, some beat-up cowboy boots or a little sequinned 1940s hat like the Queen wears? We're not exactly sure what C was on, but her flashback threads sure are trippy. There's another branch in **Newtown** (☎ 9585 4343; 180 King St).

SEDITION *Music*

☎ 9331 8832; 275 Victoria St, Darlinghurst; ⏱ 9am-6pm Mon-Sat; 🚇 Kings Cross 🚌 323-7, 324-5, 333
Michael the barber will give you a $20 short back 'n' sides while you give jazz, reggae and classic rock records a try-before-you-buy listen and attempt to ignore the wall of '60s *Playboy* centrefolds. He also sells weird books, cult videos and other kooky stuff – maybe a 'How to Play Banjo' guide is up your alley.

WHEELS & DOLL BABY *Fashion*

☎ 9361 3286; www.wheelsanddollbaby .com; 259 Crown St, Darlinghurst;

KINGS CROSS, DARLINGHURST & AROUND

⊙ 10am-6pm Mon-Wed, Fri & Sat, to 8pm Thu, noon-5pm Sun; 🚆 Museum Ⓜ World Square 🚌 308-10, 343 'Clothes to snare a millionaire' is the name of the game here, and what a wicked, wicked game it is. Lace, leather and leopard-print; studs, suspenders and satin. Tight-wrapped and trussed-up, it won't just be the millionaires who'll be looking your way.

🍴 EAT

🍴 A TAVOLA *Italian* $$

☎ 9331 7871; www.atavola.com.au; 348 Victoria St, Darlinghurst; ⊙ noon-3pm Fri, 6-10pm Mon-Sat; 🚆 Kings Cross

This is the best pasta you'll ever have (we're serious…forget Napoli). The menu will only have three or four dishes to choose from, but they'll all be fantastic. Don't be afraid to bump elbows with your co-diners at the long communal table.

🍴 AKI'S *Indian* $$

☎ 9332 4600; www.akisindian.com.au; 1 The Wharf, Cowper Wharf Rd, Woolloo-mooloo; ⊙ noon-3pm Sun-Fri, 6pm-late daily; 🚌 311; ♿ Ⓥ

The first cab off the rank as you walk onto Woolloomooloo's wharf is Aki's. And you need walk no further: this is beautifully presented, intuitively constructed high-Indian cuisine, supplemented by a six-page wine list show-casing local and international drops by the glass or bottle. The Kerala chilli beef is a simmering sensation.

Caffeine junkies, get your fix at Bar Coluzzi (p102)

BAR COLUZZI *Café* $

☎ 9380 5420; 322 Victoria St, Darlinghurst; ⏰ 5am-7pm; 🚇 Kings Cross 🚍 323-7, 324-5, 389; ♿ Ⓥ

Legendary Coluzzi has been infusing Darlinghurst with caffeine for 50 years. The food is fine, but what you're here for is the spoon-standing-up-straight-in-the-cup coffee.

BILLS *Mod Oz* $$

☎ 9360 9631; www.bills.com.au; 433 Liverpool St, Darlinghurst; ⏰ 7.30am-3pm Mon-Sat, 8.30am-3pm Sun; 🚍 373, 377, 380, 389, 399; ♿ Ⓥ

Sydneysiders adore Bill Granger's sunny eatery with its large, newspaper-strewn communal table. Dishes such as sweetcorn fritters with roast tomato, spinach and bacon are equally adorable. Can't get a seat? Head for the other **branches** (Surry Hills Map p89, C3; ☎ 9360 4762; 359 Crown St; Woollahra Map p111, E3; ☎ 9328 7997; 118 Queen St).

DOV AT DELECTICA *Mod Oz* $$

☎ 9368 0600; www.cafedov.com.au; Shop 2, 130 Victoria St, Potts Point; ⏰ 7am-4pm Mon & Tue, to 10pm Wed-Sat, 8.30am-3pm Sun; 🚇 Kings Cross 🚍 323-7, 324-5, 389; Ⓥ

It's probably linked to endless nights of party-love, but big breakfasts are something Sydney does well. DOV, the busiest café on Victoria St, does one of the best.

If they sleep through breakfast, locals, backpackers, style-mongers and filmmakers squish in for lunch and dinner. The DOV burger reigns supreme.

FISH FACE *Seafood* $$

☎ 9332 4803; www.fishface.com.au; 132 Darlinghurst Rd, Darlinghurst; ⏰ 6-10pm Mon-Sat, 6-9pm Sun; 🚇 Kings Cross

This unassuming-looking, tiled, triangular fish-and-chipper has a magical menu: stylin' sushi, amazing fish curries and upbeat underwater species such as Hiramasa kingfish with spiced beetroot relish and crispy pancetta. The kitchen takes up most of the space – stools and benches are an afterthought.

FRATELLI PARADISO *Italian* $$

☎ 9357 1744; 12-16 Challis Ave, Potts Point; ⏰ 7.30am-10pm Mon-Fri, 7am-6pm Sat & Sun; 🚇 Kings Cross 🚍 311; ♿ Ⓥ

This stylish bistro-bakery has them queuing at the door (especially on weekends). The intimate, mod room showcases seasonal Italian dishes cooked with Mediterranean zing. Lots of busy black-clad waiters, lots of Italian chatter, lots of oversized sunglasses – somehow Rome doesn't seem so far away… No bookings.

🍴 HARRY'S CAFÉ DE WHEELS
Café $

☎ 9357 3074; www.harryscafedewheels
.com.au; Cowper Wharf Rd, Wooloo-
mooloo; ⏱ 9am-1am Mon-Wed, to 3am
Thu, to 4am Fri & Sat, to midnight Sun;
🚌 311; ♿ 👶

For over 70 years (!), cab drivers,
sailors and boozed-up noc-
turnals have slurred orders for
pea-and-pie floaters over Harry's
famous counter. Sit on a milk crate
overlooking the hulking Wooloo-
mooloo warships and gulp down a
'Tiger' (pie, peas, mashed potatoes
and gravy). Deadly.

🍴 HUGO'S BAR PIZZA
Italian $$

☎ 9357 4018; www.hugos.com.au;
33 Bayswater Rd, Kings Cross; ⏱ 5pm-
2am Mon-Sat, 3pm-2am Sun; 🚆 Kings
Cross 🚌 323-7, 324-5, 333; ♿ Ⓥ

Sassy little brother of Hugo's
Lounge upstairs (p104), this indoor/
outdoor neighbourhood nook
has been seducing pizza fans with
its delicious discs and home-style
Italian fare. The marble-fronted bar
and sunken velvet lounge spell
luxury, but the menu won't break
the bank. Try the *puttanesca* pizza.

🍴 LIBERTINE
Mod Oz & Southeast Asian $$$

☎ 9368 7507; www.libertine.net.au;
1 Kellett St, Kings Cross; ⏱ 6-11pm;
🚆 Kings Cross 🚌 323-7, 324-5, 333; Ⓥ

Libertine means 'morally dis-
solute'. Check your moral fibre
at the door of this luxuriant,
unrestrained wonderland – gold
and crimson drapes, lacquered
black timbers and chandeliers set
the scene for captivating fusion
dishes such as the house curry
(green prawns, squid and butter-
nut pumpkin). Cement your moral
decay at the cocktail bar.

🍴 OTTO *Italian* $$$

☎ 9368 7488; www.otto.net.au;
8 The Wharf, Cowper Wharf Rd, Woolloomooloo; ⏱ noon-midnight; 🚌 311;
♿ Ⓥ

Forget the glamorous waterfront
location and A-list crowd – what
Otto will be remembered for is
single-handedly dragging Sydney's Italian cooking into the new
century. Dishes like *strozzapreti
con gamberi* (artisan pasta with
fresh Yamba prawns, tomato,
chilli and black olives) define
culinary perfection. Bookings
essential.

🍴 YELLOW *Mod Oz & Deli* $$

☎ 9357 3400; www.ycook.com.au; 57-
59 Macleay St, Potts Point; ⏱ 7.30am-
6pm Sun & Mon, to 9.30pm Tue-Sat;
🚆 Kings Cross 🚌 311; ♿ 👶 Ⓥ

Yes indeed, it's yellow. The
cheeriness continues inside
where bouncy/touchy/feely staff
enthusiastically proffer the finest

olive oils, homemade pastas, cakes, quiches, jam, polenta and sausages. The bistro next door throws it all together and comes up with winners. Hey, is that Paul Keating in the corner?

☒ ZINC *Café* $$

☎ 9358 6777; zincbar@ihug.com.au; 77 Macleay St, Potts Point; ☼ 7am-4pm daily, 6.30-11pm Tue-Sat; ☒ Kings Cross ☒ 311; Ⓥ

Zinc's good-looking staff are full of smiles; maybe the new dinner shifts agree with them. But Zinc was built on breakfasts, and the kitchen continues to create too many hard decisions for 8am. The pancakes with ricotta and berry compote, or eggs with sugar-cured salmon? Both.

☿ DRINK
☒ DARLO BAR *Pub*

☎ 9331 3672; www.darlobar.com.au; Royal Sovereign Hotel, 306 Liverpool St, Darlinghurst; admission free; ☼ 10am-midnight Mon-Sat, noon-midnight Sun; ☒ Kings Cross ☒ 323-7, 324-5, 333, 389;

The Darlo's triangular retro room is a magnet for thirsty urban bohemians with something to read or a hankering for pinball or pool. Afterwards, they roll down the hill to the beer garden at the Green Park Hotel (right).

☒ GAZEBO WINE GARDEN
Wine Bar

☎ 9357 5333; www.gazebowinegarden.com.au; 2 Elizabeth Bay Rd, Elizabeth Bay; ☼ 3pm-midnight Mon-Thu, noon-midnight Fri-Sun; ☒ Kings Cross

A hip wine bar in skanky old Fitzroy Gardens? Who would have believed it 10 years ago? This place is awesome – supergroovy décor (wrought-iron gates, bespoke benches, eclectic couches), interesting gay/straight drinkers and 55 sometimes obscure wines available by the glass (plus 300 by the bottle).

☒ GREEN PARK HOTEL *Pub*

☎ 9380 5311; www.solotel.com.au; 360 Victoria St, Darlinghurst; admission free; ☼ 10am-2am Mon-Fri, noon-2am Sat & Sun; ☒ 373, 377, 380, 389, 399

The ever-rockin' Green Park has pool tables, a beer garden with funky Dr Seuss–inspired lighting and a huge central bar teeming with travellers, gays and pierced locals. Bowie and Queen rule the jukebox.

☒ HUGO'S LOUNGE *Bar*

☎ 9357 4411; www.hugos.com.au; L1, 33 Bayswater Rd, Kings Cross; Thu admission free, Fri-Sun $10; ☼ 5.30pm-3am Thu-Sat, 8pm-3am Sun; ☒ Kings Cross ☒ 323-7, 324-5, 333

Upper-crust interiors attract a glossy crowd of media celebs con-

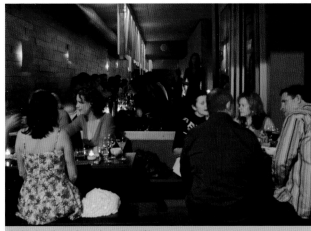
Drink in the understated atmosphere at Jimmy Lik's

ducting histrionic conversations in between mobile-phone calls. If it feels like a CD launch you weren't invited to, head to the terrace for a stiff drink or Hugo's Bar Pizza (p103) downstairs for some tasty respite.

☑ JIMMY LIK'S *Bar*
☎ 8354 1400; www.jimmyliks.com; 186 Victoria St, Potts Point; admission free; ☀ 5pm-midnight; 🚇 Kings Cross 🚌 323-7, 324-5, 333
Understated and subtle, Jimmy's is very cool, with benches almost as long as the cocktail list (try a Thai-hewn Mekong Mary with chilli lime sauce). Jimmy's Thai restaurant is next door – there's usually a wait for a seat, but with tasty bar snacks available, what's the hurry?

☑ OLD FITZROY HOTEL *Pub*
☎ 9356 3848; www.oldfitzroy.com.au; 129 Dowling St, Woolloomooloo; ☀ 11am-midnight Mon-Fri, noon-midnight Sat, 3-10pm Sun; 🚇 Kings Cross 🚌 311, 323-7, 324-5, 333
Is it a pub? A theatre? A bistro? Actually it's all three. Grab a bowl of laksa, assess the acting talent of tomorrow and wash it all down with a beer ($35 for the lot). The outdoor deck is unbeatable on a steamy summer night.

▼ OXFORD HOTEL *Pub*

☎ 9331 3467; www.theoxfordhotel
.com.au; 134 Oxford St, Darlinghurst;
admission free; 🕑 24hr downstairs, Gilligan's 5pm-late, Supper Club 7pm-late
Wed-Sun; 🚌 378, 380, 389
Big and beige, the ever-lovin'
Oxford is a Taylor Sq beacon.
Downstairs it's beer-swilling and
mannish. Basement-level Gilligan's
is a hip club; the 1st-floor Supper
Club has indulgent lounge service.
Post-dance-party crowds heave
and sway. Wheelchair access
downstairs only.

▼ RUBY RABBIT *Bar*

☎ 9332 3197; www.rubyrabbit.com.au;
231 Oxford St, Darlinghurst; admission
free-$15; 🕑 9pm-late Thu-Sun; 🚌 378,
380, 389
Wow! What a cool bar. The own-
ers have spared no expense on
the interiors, coming up with a
design best described as Alice in
Wonderland tickles Austin Powers
while kissing Britt Ekland in the
Palace of Versailles (if you know
what we mean). Damn funky, and
damn difficult to get into – dress
to the nines.

▼ TILBURY HOTEL *Pub*

☎ 9368 1955; www.tilburyhotel.com
.au; 12-18 Nicholson St, Woolloomooloo;
admission free; 🕑 8am-midnight
Mon-Fri, from 9am Sat, from 10am Sun;
🚌 311

Once the dank domain of burly
sailors and salty ne'er-do-wells,
the Tilbury now sparkles on
Sydney's social scene. Yuppies,
yachties, suits, gays and straights
populate the light, bright interiors.
The bistro and beer garden are
packed on weekends, and sailors
can still get a beer.

▼ VICTORIA ROOM *Bar*

☎ 9357 4488; www.thevictoriaroom
.com; L1, 235 Victoria St, Darlinghurst;
admission free; 🕑 6pm-midnight Tue-
Thu, to 2am Fri & Sat, 2pm-midnight Sun;
🚈 Kings Cross 🚌 323-7, 324-5, 333, 389
Plush chesterfields, Art Nouveau
wallpaper, dark-wood panelling
and bamboo screens – the Victoria
Room is the spoilt love child of a
1920s Bombay gin palace and a
Hong Kong opium den. Don your
white linen suit and panama and
order a Raspberry Debonair at
the bar.

▼ WATER BAR *Bar*

☎ 9331 9000; www.tajhotels.com
/sydney; BLUE Sydney, 6 Cowper Wharf
Rd, Woolloomooloo; admission free;
🕑 4pm-midnight Tue-Sat, to 10pm Sun
& Mon; 🚌 311; ♿
Time is meaningless and escape
is pointless here (especially after a
few martinis). The lofty, romantic
space sucks you in to its pink-love
world of candles, corners, deep
lounges and ottomans as big as
beds. Great for business (if you
really must), but better for lurve.

NEIGHBOURHOODS

KINGS CROSS, DARLINGHURST & AROUND

PLAY

⭐ ARQ *Club*

☎ 9380 8700; www.arqsydney.com.au; 16 Flinders St, Darlinghurst; admission free-$20, Thu free; ✹ 9pm-late Thu-Sun; 🚌 378, 380, 389; ♿

If Noah had to fill his Arq with groovy, gay clubbers, he'd head here with a big net and some tranquillisers. This flash megaclub has a cocktail bar, recovery room and two dance floors with high-energy House, drag shows and a hyperactive smoke machine.

⭐ BAR ME & EL ROCCO JAZZ CELLAR *Live Music*

☎ 9368 0894; 154 Brougham St, Kings Cross; admission free-$10; ✹ 5pm-1am Mon-Fri, 6pm-1am Sat & Sun; 🚇 Kings Cross

Between 1955 and 1969 this was Sydney's premier finger-snappin', beret-wearing boho dive, hosting performances by Frank Sinatra and Sarah Vaughan. Those heady days are long gone, but live jazz is back on the agenda in the legendary rock-hewn basement. Free open-mic nights fortnightly on Mondays.

⭐ CANDYS APARTMENT *Club*

☎ 9380 5600; www.candys.com.au; 22 Bayswater Rd, Kings Cross; admission $10-15; ✹ 8pm-late Thu-Sun; 🚇 Kings

Cross 🚌 323-7, 324-5, 333

An unpretentious, grungy club, unique in its decision to let ugly people in the door. The music is good and no-one really bothers about anything other than having a few drinks, a dance and a good time. Occasional live acts.

⭐ DARLINGHURST THEATRE COMPANY *Theatre*

☎ 8356 9987; www.darlinghursttheatre.com; 19 Greenknowe Ave, Potts Point; tickets $37/32; ✹ box office 6-10pm Tue-Sat, 4-7pm Sun; 🚇 Kings Cross 🚌 311

The DTC brings clever, pithy and intelligent Australian scripts to life in its intimate (and allegedly haunted!) Potts Point theatre. The theatre features seats, dressing room mirrors, lighting and the original bar top from the old Her Majesty's Theatre in Haymarket.

⭐ EXCHANGE HOTEL *Club*

☎ 9331 2956; www.pashpresents.com; 34-44 Oxford St, Darlinghurst; admission Q bar free-$20, Spectrum $7-25, Phoenix $5-10, Exchange free; ✹ Q Bar & Phoenix 10pm-late Wed-Sun, Spectrum 8pm-late Wed-Sun, Exchange 10am-4am Mon-Fri, 9am-6am Sat & Sun; 🚇 Museum 🚌 378, 380, 389

There's a whole mess of venues here, mashed together under one roof: Q Bar pumps hot House seven nights a week; Spectrum is an alt-indie club with live bands; sticky,

Tacky and seedy just add to the vibe at Kings Cross

sexy, claustrophobic Phoenix is home to alternative gay clubbers. Sandwiched in between, the Exchange is a regulation beery pub.

⭐ MIDNIGHT SHIFT *Club*

☎ 9360 4319; www.themidnightshift
.com; 85 Oxford St, Darlinghurst; admission video bar free, club $5-25; ⏱ video bar noon-late Mon-Sat, from 3pm Sun, club 11pm-late Fri & Sat; 🚇 Museum 🚌 378, 380, 389

Sydney's perennial good-time boy palace packs in everyone from beefcakes to drags. The grog is cheap, the patrons messy, Kylie rules and mankind chalks its collective cue by the pool tables. Pick up a pick-up card at the bar to help with introductions ('I'm easy…but it looks like you're hard…').

⭐ SLIDE *Club*

☎ 8915 1899; www.slide.com.au; 41 Oxford St, Darlinghurst; admission Wed & Thu free, Fri/Sat after 10pm $5/10; ⏱ 7pm-late Wed-Sun; 🚌 Museum 🚌 378, 380, 389; ♿

Slide inside Slide, a gorgeously converted banking chamber where a colourful crowd of sexy gays and straights shimmy across polished concrete between plush booths and the central bar. If the sound and vision overwhelms, spy yourself a candidate from the mezzanine.

⭐ STABLES THEATRE *Theatre*
☎ 8002 4772, tickets 1300 306 776;
www.griffintheatre.com.au; 10 Nimrod
St, Darlinghurst; tickets $44/33; ⏱ box
office 1hr before shows; 🚇 Kings Cross
🚌 323-7, 324-5, 333, 389

In the 19th century this place was
knee-high in horse dung; now it's
home to the critically acclaimed
Griffin Theatre Co, dedicated
to nurturing new writers and
performing experimental works
by contemporary Australian play-
wrights. Book online, by phone or
at the box office an hour before
the show.

⭐ STONEWALL HOTEL *Club*
☎ 9360 1963; www.stonewallhotel
.com; 175 Oxford St, Darlinghurst;
admission free; ⏱ 11am-6am; 🚌 378,
380, 389

Nicknamed 'Stonehenge' by
those who think it's archaic (gay
druids?), the Stonewall has three
levels of bars and dance floors.
Cabaret, karaoke and games
nights spice things up – Wednesday's 'Malebox' is a sure-fire way
to bag yourself a boy.

⭐ SYDNEY BY DIVA
Organised Tour
☎ 9360 5557; www.sydneybydiva.com
.au; tours depart Oxford Hotel, Taylor Sq,
Darlinghurst; tours $100; ⏱ 6pm & 8pm
subject to minimum bookings; 🚌 378,
380, 389

All aboard for a truly camp, three-
hour, 'rosé-tinted' drag queen
comic tour of Sydney, taking in
the Opera House, Bondi Beach
and a drag show at the Imperial
Hotel, home of *Priscilla, Queen of
the Desert*.

⭐ TONIC LOUNGE *Club*
☎ 8354 1544; www.toniclounge.com
.au; 62-64 Kellett St, Kings Cross;
admission $5-10; ⏱ 9pm-late Fri-Sun;
🚇 Kings Cross 🚌 323-7, 324-5, 333

Just the tonic for snooty Sydney –
a laid-back, clubby boudoir in a
black-and-purple terrace house
that feels more like someone's
living room than anything hi-tech
or *haute couture*. The fact that
it's so un-Sydney attracts people
who are also un-Sydney – expect
backpackers aplenty.

⭐ YU *Club*
☎ 9358 65117; www.yu.com.au; 171
Victoria St, Potts Point; admission Fri/Sat/
Sun $15/20/10; ⏱ 10pm-6am Fri-Sun;
🚇 Kings Cross 🚌 323-7, 324-5, 333

Debut the sassy new eastern
suburbs you at Yu. Sydney's best
House DJs and vocal MCs spin
hip-hop, nu-skool, vocal and funky
House in three rooms divided by
sliding video screens. 'Piccadilly
Sundays' sessions kick till you can't
take no mo'. Upstairs is Soho Bar
– an Art Deco space where visiting
celebs like to shoot pool.

>PADDINGTON & WOOLLAHRA

Paddington, aka 'Paddo', is a steep, leafy suburb of restored terrace houses. Rugged bushland until the 1860s, Paddo was built for aspiring Victorian artisans, but after WWII it became Australia's worst slum. In the 1960s, renewed passion for Victorian architecture dragged Paddington back from the brink; by the '90s, real estate was out of reach for all but the lucky and the loaded.

Today, fashionable types drift between Oxford St's designer shops, chic restaurants and galleries. The suburb's flamboyant spirit comes courtesy of a vibrant gay community; Taylor Sq on Oxford St is gay Sydney's decadent nucleus. Just north of Oxford St is Five Ways, a neighbourhood hotspot. At the eastern end of Oxford St is Centennial Park, Sydney's biggest park.

Woollahra is upper-crust Sydney at its finest. Leafy streets, mansions, wall-to-wall BMWs and expensive antique shops. Maybe this is your bag; maybe it isn't – whatever your inclination, spending an afternoon here is socially enlightening.

PADDINGTON & WOOLLAHRA

NEIGHBOURHOODS

PADDINGTON & WOOLLAHRA

SEE

AUSTRALIAN CENTRE FOR PHOTOGRAPHY
☎ 9332 1455; www.acp.au.com; 257 Oxford St, Paddington; admission free; ☼ noon-7pm Tue-Fri, 10am-6pm Sat & Sun

The nonprofit ACP exhibits the photographic gems of renowned Sydney and international photographers. It's particularly passionate about photomedia, video and digital imaging works, its displays extending into a multi-exhibition space next door.

AUSTRALIAN GALLERIES
☎ 9360 5177; www.australiangalleries .com.au; 15 Roylston St, Paddington; admission free; ☼ 10am-6pm Mon-Sat; 🚌 378, 380, 389

Contemporary Australian painting and sculpture for cashed-up collectors; A-list artists have been jostling to hang their wares here for 50 years. Works on paper feature at the **Glenmore Rd branch** (☎ 9380 8744; 24 Glenmore Rd; ☼ 10am-6pm Tue-Sat, noon-5pm Sun).

CERAMIC ART GALLERY
☎ 9361 5286; 120 Glenmore Rd, Paddington; admission free; ☼ 11am-5pm Thu-Mon; 🚌 378, 380, 389

Pushing clay to its rightful extremes (is there anything else as deliciously malleable?), exhibits at the Ceramic Art Gallery range from exquisite bowls and eggshell-thin vases to slabs of abstract madness worth starting conversations over.

HOGARTH GALLERIES
☎ 9360 6839; www.aboriginalart centres.com; 7 Walker La, Paddington; admission free; ☼ 10am-5pm Tue-Sat; 🚌 378, 380, 389

A cultural beacon in an obscure Paddington laneway, Hogarth has supported and promoted Aboriginal art since 1972. Honouring established artists and sourcing up-and-comers, Hogarth exhibits contemporary dot paintings, basketry, framed prints, fabrics, spears and didgeridoos.

IAIN DAWSON GALLERY
☎ 9358 4337; www.iaindawson.com; 72a Windsor St, Paddington; ☼ 10am-6pm Tue-Sat; 🚌 378, 380, 389; ♿

A hip new backstreet gallery – just what the Paddo art scene needed! Iain Dawson specialises in emerging Australian and Southeast Asian artists including Hugh Ford and Anna Lochtenberg Williams. Sculptors, photographers, painters and screen printers – buy 'em up now before they crack the big time.

NEILD AVENUE MAZE
☎ 9391 7000; cnr Neild Ave & Gosbell St, Paddington; admission free; 🚌 378, 380, 389; ♿

This tiny maze of impeccably trimmed, thigh-high hedges hides behind a gargantuan plane tree on a Paddington back street, squished into a cranny between a gallery and someone's back fence. It mightn't take you forever to find your way through, but it'll add a smile to your day.

☺ VICTORIA BARRACKS

☎ 9339 3170; www.awm.gov.au; cnr Oxford St & Greens Rd, Paddington; tour free, museum $2/1; ☼ tour 10am Thu, museum 10am-4pm Thu & Sun, closed Dec-Feb; ☎ 378, 380, 389; ♿
A manicured malarial vision from the peak of the British Empire, these Georgian buildings have been called the finest in the colonies. Thursday's tour takes in a flag-raising ceremony, marching band (subject to availability) and the paraphernalia-packed war museum.

☺ WAGNER ART GALLERY

☎ 9360 6069; www.wagnerartgallery .com.au; 39 Gurner St, Paddington; admission free; ☼ 10.30am-6pm Mon-Sat, 1-6pm Sun; ☎ 378, 380, 389
Think Boyd, Lindsay, Nolan and Friend. Think top dollar. Think champagne, turtlenecked, lah-de-dah openings (6pm to 8pm one Tuesday per month). Wagner is one of the oldest galleries in Paddington, its maturity reflected

in its composed atmosphere and high-brow decency.

SHOP

☐ ARIEL Bookshop

☎ 9332 4581; www.arielbooks.com .au; 42 Oxford St, Paddington; ☼ 9am-midnight; ☎ 378, 380, 389
Furtive artists, photographers, architects and students roam Ariel's aisles late into the night. 'Under-culture' is the thrust here – glossy art, film, fashion and design books, along with kids' books, travel guides and a queer literature section. Browse before a movie at the Academy Twin Cinema (p120) across the road.

☐ BELINDA Fashion

☎ 9387 8728; www.belinda.com.au; 39 William St, Paddington; ☼ 10am-6pm Mon-Sat, noon-5pm Sun; ☎ 378, 380, 389
Belinda stocks a tightly edited collection of Australian designers and expensive international imports. Its second, mildly less wallet-threatening store the **Corner Shop** (☎ 9380 9828; 43 William St, Paddington) is a treasure-trove of funky Australian stuff.

☐ BERKELOUW BOOKS
Bookshop

☎ 9360 3200; www.berkelouw.com.au; 19 Oxford St, Paddington; ☼ 9am-midnight; ☎ 378, 380, 389

NEIGHBOURHOODS

PADDINGTON & WOOLLAHRA

DIVINE DESIGNERS

Paddington is ripe with fab, flimsy Australian creations for size-six disciples of inter-national style:

Bracewell (☎ 9331 5844; www.bracewell.com.au; 274 Oxford St, Paddington; ⏱ 10am-6pm Mon-Wed & Fri, to 8pm Thu, 10am-5pm Sat, noon-5pm Sun; 🚌 378, 380, 389) Sexy, structured and sassy; Mavi, Costume National and Paul Smith.

Lisa Ho (☎ 9327 6300; www.lisaho.com.au; 43 Queen St, Woollahra ; ⏱ 10am-6pm Mon-Wed & Sat, to 8pm Thu, 11am-5pm Sun; 🚌 378, 380, 389) Sheer party frocks for the social whirlwind that is your life.

Morrissey (☎ 9380 7422; www.morrissey-aust.com.au; 372 Oxford St, Paddington; ⏱ 10am-6pm Mon-Wed & Sat, to 8pm Thu, 11am-5pm Sun; 🚌 378, 380, 389) Attention high-heeled amber-tan babes: bring your gold credit card.

Expecting the dank aroma of second-hand books? Forget it! Follow your nose up to the café, then browse through three floors of preloved tomes, new releases, antique maps and Australia's largest collection of rare books. Also in **Newtown** (Map p77, C5; ☎ 9557 1777; 6-8 O'Connell St) and **Leichhardt** (off Map p77; ☎ 9560 3200; 70 Norton St).

🏠 CALIBRE Fashion
☎ 9380 5993; www.calibreclothing.com.au; 398 Oxford St, Paddington; ⏱ 9.30am-6pm Mon-Wed & Sat, to 8pm Thu, 10am-6pm Sat, 11am-5pm Sun; 🚌 378, 380, 389
Hip, high-calibre Calibre fills the wardrobes of Sydney's power players with schmick suits in seasonal fabrics and colours, plus Gucci sunnies, Costume National shoes, YSL ties and Samsonite briefcases. Gordon Gecko eat your heart out.

🏠 COLLETTE DINNIGAN Fashion
☎ 9360 6691; www.collettedinnigan.com; 33 William St, Paddington; ⏱ 10am-6pm Mon-Sat, noon-5pm Sun; 🚌 378, 380, 389
This shop's sanded floors, French drapes and wrought-iron staircase are a sexy backdrop for Collette Dinnigan's flouncy beaded dresses. Hollywood's Aussie gals flock here whenever they need a new frock (Nicole or Naomi might be in the next change room).

🏠 DINOSAUR DESIGNS Jewellery
☎ 9361 3776; www.dinosaurdesigns.com.au; 339 Oxford St, Paddington; ⏱ 10am-6pm Mon-Wed, Fri & Sat, to 7pm Thu, 11am-5pm Sun; 🚌 378, 380, 389
If Fred and Barney opened a jewellery store, this is what it would look

like. Oversized, jewel-coloured, translucent-resin bangles and baubles sit among technicoloured vases and bowls and chunky sterling-silver rings and necklaces.

☐ FOLKWAYS *Music*
☎ 9361 3980; info@folkways.com.au; 282 Oxford St, Paddington; ⌚ 9am-6pm Mon-Wed & Sat, to 9pm Thu, 11am-6pm Sun; 🚌 378, 380, 389

If Mongolian throat singers rock your world, then long-established Folkways – Sydney's premier stockist of world music CDs – is your spiritual home. Expect pressings from Central Asia to the Central Australian desert and an extensive selection of jazz and blues.

☐ HERRINGBONE *Fashion*
☎ 9327 6470; www.herringbone.com; 102 Queen St, Woollahra; ⌚ 10am-6pm Mon-Wed & Fri, to 7.30pm Thu, 9am-6pm Sat, 11am-5pm Sun; 🚌 378, 380, 389

Combining Australian design with Italian fabrics, Herringbone produces something English-looking – men's and women's shirts with crisp collars and bright colours. When the stock market went south in 2008, suit sales followed, but 'bone boys have endured.

☐ JONES THE GROCER
Food & Drink
☎ 9362 1222; www.jonesthegrocer .com; 68 Moncur St, Woollahra; ⌚ 7.30am-5.30pm Mon-Sat, 9am-5pm Sun; 🚌 378, 380, 389

Bob the Builder, Jones the Grocer... some things just make sense. JTG offers high-end groceries, cookbooks and gourmet goodies galore. Munch into a caramel slice with a serious coffee at the café, then double-wrap some double brie and hotfoot it to Centennial Park for a picnic.

Sample the gourmet wares at Jones the Grocer

KIDSTUFF
Toy Shop

☎ 9363 2838; www.kidstuff.com.au;
126a Queen St, Woollahra; ⏰ 9.30am-
5.30pm Mon-Sat, 9am-5pm Sun; 🚌 378,
380, 389
Parents seem relieved to discover
this small, vaguely hippie shop
filled with educational, traditional,
low-tech toys and games. Aiming
to engage and expand kids' minds,
well-known brands mix with costumes, musical instruments, soft
toys, dolls' houses and magnetic
fridge letters (teach them how to
spell 'p-l-a-y-s-t-a-t-i-o-n').

LEE HARDCASTLE
ANTIQUES *Antiques*

☎ 9362 0935; lee.hardcastle@bigpond
.com; 28 Queen St, Woollahra; ⏰ 10am-
5pm Mon-Sat; 🚌 378, 380, 389
Bordering on bizarre, this shop
is more like a natural-history
museum than an antique dealer.
Eighteenth- and early 19th-century
taxidermy items (zebras, warthogs,
black bears and deer) jostle for position with whale ribs, grandfather
clocks and walnut wardrobes.

LEONA EDMISTON
Fashion

☎ 9331 7033; www.leonaedmiston
.com; 88 William St, Paddington;
⏰ 10am-6pm Mon-Wed & Fri, to 8pm
Thu, to 5.30pm Sat, noon-5pm Sun;
🚌 378, 380, 389

Leona Edmiston clearly knows
a thing or two about dresses.
Her sassy designs have been described as exuberantly feminine,
flirtatious and fun. They're cut
from the best cottons, silks and
jerseys in colours that range from
luscious, sophisticated reds to
pinstripes and polka dots. Also at
Strand Arcade (p40).

ORSON & BLAKE
Homewares

☎ 9326 1155; www.orsonandblake
.com.au; 83-85 Queen St, Woollahra;
⏰ 10am-5.30pm Mon-Sat, 11am-5pm
Sun; 🚌 378, 380, 389
Sydney's most stylish homewares
emporium will make your house
look cool even if you're not –
everything from notepads to
garden statues at the height of
chic. Head upstairs for clothes
by top-notch Australian and Kiwi
designers plus opulent scarves,
handbags and jewellery. Also in
Surry Hills (Map p89, B5; ☎ 8399 2525;
483 Riley St).

PADDINGTON MARKET
Market

☎ 9331 2923; www.paddingtonmarkets
.com.au; 395 Oxford St, Paddington;
⏰ 10am-4pm Sat, to 5pm summer;
🚌 378, 380, 389
Join the meandering throngs for
a foot massage, tarot reading or
funky shirt to wear clubbing that

Feminine meets fun at Leona Edmiston

night. Sydney's most-attended weekend market congregates around Paddington Uniting Church, coughing up everything from vintage clothes and hip fashions to jewellery, books, massage and palmistry. Parking is a misery here – take public transport.

SASS & BIDE *Fashion*
☎ 9360 3900; www.sassandbide.com; 132 Oxford St, Paddington; ☺ 10am-6pm Mon-Wed, Fri & Sat, to 8pm Thu, 11am-5pm Sun; 🚌 378, 380, 389 Brisbane's Heidi Middleton and Sarah-Jane Clarke got their start with a stall on London's Portobello Rd before heading

NEIGHBOURHOODS

PADDINGTON & WOOLLAHRA

to Sydney in 1999 and starting the label that's made them international stars. Come here for sass(y) low-cut women's jeans, body-hugging jackets and minidresses.

🔲 VERNE JEWELS *Jewellery*
☎ 9361 3669; vernjewels@hotmail.com; 36b Oxford St, Paddington; ☼ 10am-5pm Mon-Sat; 🚌 378, 380, 389
With an exquisite eye and a wry sense of history, Nicholas Bullough (no, he's not Verne, that's a joke – Jules Verne, get it?) assembles the artefacts, stones, pearls and gems he buys around the world and comes up with winners every time.

🍴 EAT

🍴 AMPERSAND CAFÉ & BOOKSTORE *Café* $
☎ 9380 6617; www.cafebookstore.com.au; 78 Oxford St, Paddington; ☼ 7.30am-6pm Mon-Fri, to 6.30pm Sat, 9am-6.30pm Sun; 🚌 378, 380, 389; V ♿
Which are better, books or cooks? Either way, you're guaranteed to find a good read (30,000 books over three floors) and a good coffee here. Muffins, toasted sandwiches, wraps, croissants, salads and smoothies round out the experience. Aim for one of the little orange tables in the alleyway.

🍴 ARTHUR'S PIZZA
Italian $$
☎ 9332 2220; 260 Oxford St, Paddington; ☼ 5pm-midnight Mon-Fri, noon-midnight Sat & Sun; 🚌 378, 380, 389; V ♿
For some reason Arthur's sign was originally installed upside down. Then some do-gooder turned it right-way-up. Now it's topsy-turvy again. Immune to this sign-writing schizophrenia, Art's pizzas continue to impress. Try the 'Zorro' (olives, ricotta, red onion, spinach and semidried tomato).

🍴 BISTRO MONCUR
French $$$
☎ 9363 2519; www.bistromoncur.com.au; 116 Queen St, Woollahra; ☼ noon-3pm Thu-Sun, 6-10.30pm Mon-Sat, to 9pm Sun; 🚌 378, 380, 389; V
Minimoguls and luncheon ladies while away afternoons below Bistro Moncur's vaulted ceilings and Matisse-esque murals. Dishes such as blue swimmer crab omelette are ingrained in Sydney's culinary lexicon. The wine list will make you want to take up mogulling too.

🍴 BUON RICORDO *Italian* $$$
☎ 9360 6729; www.buonricordo.com.au; 108 Boundary St, Paddington; ☼ noon-2.30pm Fri & Sat, 6.30-10.30pm Tue-Sat, supper till midnight; 🚌 378, 380, 389; V

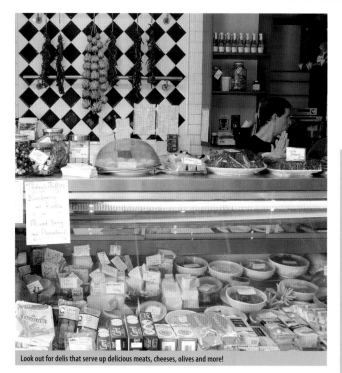

Look out for delis that serve up delicious meats, cheeses, olives and more!

Remember the good old days, when local restaurateurs knew you well enough to select your meal for you? Well, Buon Ricordo is very 'good old days'. Let bearded chef Armando Percuoco decide whether you want the *zuppa di pesce* or the *tagliata con rucola*. The best Italian in Sydney? Reservations essential.

LA GERBE D'OR
French Café $

☎ 9331 1070; 255 Glenmore Rd, Five Ways, Paddington; ⏰ 7am-7pm Tue-Fri, to 6pm Sat, to 4pm Sun; 🚌 378, 380, 389; Ⓥ ♿

Sydney's most-loved patisserie, La Gerbe d'Or (pronunciation:

with *thee*k Parisian accent) has been baking mouth-watering French breads, cakes, pastries and quiches for more than 25 years. The chunky beef-and-burgundy pies are legendary.

🍴 SUGO
Italian $$

☎ 9331 2962; www.sugo.net.au; 10 Elizabeth St, Paddington; ⏰ 6pm-midnight Mon-Thu, 6pm-late Fri & Sat; 🚌 378, 380, 389; Ⓥ

Backstreet Sugo serves a couple of sassy pastas and risottos, but the pizzas are why you're here. The Mare E Monti (prawns, zucchini, cherry tomatoes, garlic and chilli) will make you renounce chunky new-world crusts for eternity.

🍴 VAMPS BISTRO
French $$

☎ 9331 1032; www.vampsbistro.com; 227 Glenmore Rd, Paddington; ⏰ 6.30-10.30pm Tue-Fri, 9am-3pm & 6.30-10.30pm Sat, 9am-3pm Sun; 🚌 389

This romantic Five Ways Frenchie plates up classics like duck *à l'orange* and crêpe suzette, but it's the weekend breakfasts that keeps us coming back. After a hard day's night, grab a courtyard seat, order a strong coffee and vamp it up with the wait staff.

🍸 DRINK

🍸 LORD DUDLEY HOTEL *Pub*

☎ 9327 5399; www.lorddudley.com.au; 236 Jersey Rd, Woollahra; admission free; ⏰ 11am-11pm Mon-Wed, to midnight Thu-Sat, noon-10pm Sun; 🚌 378, 380, 389

Packed with poncy, scarf-wearing MG drivers and block-shouldered Rugby Union types, the Lord Dudley is as close as Sydney gets to an English pub. Dark woody walls; quality beers by the pint.

🍸 PADDINGTON INN *Pub*

☎ 9380 5277; www.paddingtoninn.com.au; 338 Oxford St, Paddington; admission free; ⏰ noon-midnight Sun-Thu, to 1am Fri & Sat; 🚌 378, 380, 389

The Paddo's exterior is painted a stylish mushroom, while inside it's all organically shaped wall nooks, stainless-steel stools and mildly sinister lighting. Good-looking locals elbow around the pool table; the restaurant serves upmarket pub grub.

⭐ PLAY

✴ ACADEMY TWIN CINEMA
Cinema

☎ 9331 3457; www.palacecinemas.com.au; 3a Oxford St, Paddington; tickets $16.50/14; ⏰ 11am-9.30pm; 🚌 378, 380, 389

Art-house enthusiasts roll up for the Academy's broad selection of independent Australian and international releases and annual Italian, Mardi Gras, French and Spanish film festivals (in February, March, April and May respectively).

✪ CHAUVEL CINEMA *Cinema*
☎ 9361 5398; www.chauvelcinema.net .au; cnr Oxford St & Oatley Rd, Paddington; tickets $16.50/14; ⏱ 1pm-midnight Mon-Fri, from 11am Sat & Sun; 🚌 378, 380, 389
Inside the historic Paddington Town Hall, the revamped Chauvel's mission statement is to offer distinct and alternative cinema experiences and to foster Sydney's film culture.

✪ HOYTS EQ *Cinema*
☎ 9332 1633; www.hoyts.com.au; Bent St, Moore Park; tickets $16.50/14; ⏱ 10.30am-midnight; 🚌 339
This hefty Entertainment Quarter movie complex has more than a dozen cinemas, including an Imax screen and 'La Premiere', the cinematic equivalent of a 1st-class cabin (movie, lounge chairs, bar access and popcorn for $33). Art-house fare screens in Cinema Paris, just down Bent St.

✪ MOONLIGHT CINEMA *Cinema*
☎ 1300 551 908; www.moonlight .com.au; Centennial Park, Oxford St, Woollahra; tickets $18/15; ⏱ dusk, late Nov-early Mar; 🚇 Bondi Junction 🚌 378, 380, 389; ♿ 🚻
A mellow way to enjoy a balmy summer evening: bring a rug, a picnic and a mate. The programme includes classics such as *Breakfast at Tiffany's*, *Ferris Bueller's Day Off* and *A Clockwork Orange*. Buy tickets online, by phone or at the gate from 7pm (subject to availability).

✪ SYDNEY COMEDY STORE *Comedy*
☎ 9357 1419; www.comedystore .com.au; Entertainment Quarter, Lang Rd, Moore Park; tickets $15-30; ⏱ box office 10am-6pm Mon, to midnight Tue-Sat; 🚌 339, 371-4, 376-7; ♿
This purpose-built comedy hall lures big-time Australian and overseas stand-ups and nurtures new talent with open-mic and 'New Comics' nights. US, Irish and Edinburgh Festival performers have 'em rolling in the aisles on a regular basis. Bookings advisable.

>BONDI, BRONTE & COOGEE

In pre-rollerblade days, the flavour of Bondi (🚌 380, 389 from Circular Quay; 🚊 Bondi Junction, then bus 381) came from Jewish, Italian and British immigrants. These days, Bondi (deriving from an Aboriginal word for the sound of the surf) is irresistibly hip – surfers, models, skate punks and tourists surf hedonistically through Campbell Pde's pubs, bars and restaurants. Housing prices on Bondi's treeless slopes have skyrocketed, but the beach remains a priceless constant.

Further south is Bronte (🚌 378 from Railway Sq, via Bondi Junction), a steep-sided beach suburb. The swimming is good, as is the collection of low-key, breezy eateries in what was once an exceedingly uncool shopping strip.

Coogee (🚌 373, 374 from Circular Quay, 372 from Railway Sq; 🚊 Bondi Junction, then bus 313, 314, 353) is further south again, a spacious, popular 'burb that's far enough from the city to be almost self sufficient – beery backpackers fill the Thai takeaways and pubs.

For more on these beaches, see p15. See also the Clifftop Trail (p140).

BONDI, BRONTE & COOGEE

👁 SEE
Bondi Pavilion 1 E2

🏠 SHOP
Bondi Markets 2 E1
Jurlique 3 D2
Zabriskie Booksellers 4 D2

🍴 EAT
Barzura 5 B8
Blue Orange 6 D2

Bondi Social 7 D2
Earth Food Store 8 D2
Gelbison 9 D2
Gertrude & Alice 10 D2
Icebergs 11 E3
Jed's Food Store 12 D1
Mongers 13 D2
Nick's 14 E2
North Bondi Italian
   Food 15 F2
Swell 16 C5

🍸 DRINK
Beach Road Hotel 17 D1
Coogee Bay Hotel 18 B8
Mocean 19 D3

⭐ PLAY
Bondi Openair
   Cinema ....(see 1)
Dive Centre Bondi 20 C2
Let's Go Surfing 21 F2
Night Cat tours 22 A3

Please see over for map

SEE

BONDI PAVILION

☎ 8362 3400; www.waverley.nsw.gov
.au/info/pavilion; Queen Elizabeth Dr,
Bondi; admission free; 🕙 10am-6pm;
🚌 381 from Bondi Junction, 380, 389
More cultural centre than boat
shed, the 1929 Mediterranean/
Georgian-revival Bondi Pavilion has
change rooms, showers, outdoor
cinema (p131), restaurants, exhibitions, courses and performances.

SHOP

BONDI MARKETS *Market*
☎ 9315 8988; www.bondimarkets
.com.au; Bondi Beach Public School, cnr
Campbell Pde & Warners Ave, Bondi;

WORTH THE TRIP
North of Bondi in Vaucluse is Sydney's
last remaining 19th-century harbourside estate, **Vaucluse House** (☎ 9388
7922; www.hht.net.au; Wentworth Rd,
Vaucluse; admission $8/4; 🕙 10am-
4.30pm Tue-Sun; 🚌 325). Built
in 1828, it's an imposing, turreted
specimen of Gothic Australiana on
10 hectares of lush gardens. Political sabre-rattler and explorer William
Charles Wentworth and his family lived
here from 1828 to 1862. Wheelchair access to ground floor only.

🕙 9am-4pm Sun; 🚌 381 from Bondi
Junction, 380, 389
Remember the days of the old
school yard? We used to laugh a

To market, to market: browse the goods at funky Bondi Markets

SOUTH
PACIFIC
OCEAN

Shark
Point

Burrows
Park

Calga
Reserve

Waverley
Cemetery

Park La

Warner La

Park La

Shakel Ave

Eastbourne Ave

Surfside Ave

Andrew St

Clovelly
Beach

Clovelly

Melrose Pde

Gordons
Bay

Boundary St

Keith St

Trafalgar St

Boundary St

Raby St

St Thomas St

Busby La

Battery St

Dunningham
Reserve

MacPherson St

Chesterfield Pde

Marloo St

Clifton Rd

Burnie St

Boundary St

Beach St

Moore St

Arcadia St

Coogee
Beach

Coogee
Bay

Carlton St

Vale St

Knox St

Greville St

Clovelly Rd

Dans Ave

Division St

Arden St

Coogee

Hill St

Coogee
Oval

Grant
Reserve

Arden St

Alfreda St

Vicar St

18

5

Yarna
Park

Wallace St

Yarna St

Barry St

Fern St

Bishops Ave

Allison Rd

Brook St

Bardon
Park

Dolphin St

Mount St

Coogee Bay Rd

Kidman St

Waltham St

Havelock Ave

Hooper St

Douglas St

Raby La

Carrington Rd

Marcel Ave

Ritchard Ave

Pauling Ave

Melody St

Abbott St

Bream St

Mount St

Byron St

Car St

0   300 m
0   0.2 miles

lot… The kids are at the beach on Sundays while their school fills up with Bondi groovers rummaging through funky second-hand clothes and books, hippy beads and earrings, aromatherapy oils, candles, old Cat Stevens records…

📖 ZABRISKIE BOOKSELLERS
Bookshop

☎ 9365 1482; www.zabriskiebooks.com; 3 Hall St, Bondi; 🕑 10am-8pm Sun-Wed, 10am-10pm Thu-Sat; 🚌 381 from Bondi Junction, 380, 389

Do bushy-bushy blonde surfies read books? If the crowds at Zabriskie's are anything to go by, the answer must be yes. This tiny cultural oasis in Bondi's literary desert has more books than space – staff scramble up ladders to get to the top shelves.

EAT

🍴 BARZURA
Café $$

☎ 9665 5546; www.barzura.com.au; 64 Carr St, Coogee; 🕑 7am-11pm; 🚌 353 from Bondi Junction, 372-4, 313-4; ♿ Ⓥ

Frequented by retired Australian cricketers in dark sunglasses, Barzura's views have to be the best of any café in Sydney (if not the world!). The sunbaked stretch north along Coogee Beach to

Bondi is a stunner, as are the deliciously uncomplicated salads, pides, pasta dishes and generous breakfasts, all served with a smile.

🍴 BLUE ORANGE
Mod Oz & Café $$

☎ 9300 9885; www.blueorangerestaurant.com.au; 49 Hall St, Bondi; 🕑 7am-4.30pm Wed-Sun, 6.30-10.30pm Wed-Sat; 🚌 381 from Bondi Junction, 380, 389; ♿ Ⓥ

A fave with Hall St regulars and travellers alike, Blue Orange has a casual, sandy vibe and a silly name, belying its delicate, complex cooking. Start with the blue cheese and walnut brûlée, then savour the slow-cooked Flinders Island lamb with roasted eggplant, fetta and mint. Divine.

🍴 BONDI SOCIAL
Mod Oz $$$

☎ 9365 1788; www.bondisocial.com; L1, 38 Campbell Pde, Bondi; 🕑 noon-late Mon-Fri, 9am-late Sat & Sun; 🚌 381 from Bondi Junction, 380, 389; ♿ Ⓥ

This cosy, chocolate-coloured, beach-shaped room opens onto a deck, from which Pacific views extend to eternity. Try the honey-glazed duck with coriander or the seared yellowfin tuna with paprika, fennel and salmon caviar. It also has a mean cocktail menu if you'd rather just sip and stare.

Icebergs (p128) is a room with a view

🍴 EARTH FOOD STORE
Café & Deli $

☎ 9365 5098; 81a Gould St, Bondi;
🕙 7am-7pm; 🚍 381 from Bondi Junction, 380, 389; ♿ ♨ Ⓥ

An organic café, deli and naturopath under one roof, this feel-good eatery plates up a healthy range of salads, quiches, sushi, lasagne, paninis, slices and tennis-ball-sized felafels, plus takeaway nuts, herbs, spices, teas, fruit-and-veg and fresh-cut flowers. The Van Morrison soundtrack keeps everyone feeling chipper.

🍴 GELBISON *Italian* $

☎ 9130 4042; fax 9300 9041; 10 Lamrock Ave, Bondi; 🕙 5-11pm; 🚍 381 from Bondi Junction, 380, 389; ♨ Ⓥ

Legendary enough for a local rock band to name themselves after it, Gelbison entertains families, backpackers, locals and visiting movie stars (is Gelbison almost an anagram for Mel Gibson?) with great-value pizza and pasta. Sit with the surfers over a steaming bowl of prawn and mushroom fettuccine or a 'magic boot' pizza.

🍴 GERTRUDE & ALICE
Café $

☎ 9130 5155; www.gertrudeandalice .com.au; 46 Hall St, Bondi; 🕙 7.30am-10pm; 🚍 381 from Bondi Junction, 380, 389; Ⓥ ♨

This second-hand bookshop-café is so un-Bondi – there's not a

WORTH THE TRIP

It's been the king of Sydney seafood for so long, you might think **Doyles on the Beach** (☎ 9337 2007; www.doyles .com.au; 11 Marine Pde, Watsons Bay; ☼ noon-3pm & 6-9pm; ⚋ Watsons Bay 🚢 325; 🚹) is resting on its laurels. Nevertheless, it isn't your average fish and chipper, and catching the harbour ferry to Watsons Bay for a seafood lunch is a quintessential Sydney experience.

model or surfer in sight! Students and academics hang out reading, sipping chai tea and acting like Americans in Paris. Join them for lentil stew and theological discussion around communal tables in shambolic book-lined rooms.

🍴 ICEBERGS
Modern Mediterranean $$$

☎ 9365 9000; www.idrb.com; 1 Notts Ave, Bondi; ☼ noon-midnight Tue-Sat, to 10pm Sun; 🚌 381 from Bondi Junction, 380, 389; 🚹 🅥

Poised above the famous swimming pool, Icebergs' views sweep across the Bondi Beach arc to the sea. Jacketed, bow-tied waiters deliver fresh seafood and steaks cooked with élan. The wine list is superb, and the bar, overlooking the Campbell Pde lights, is never a boring place for a beer. Bow down and feign humility before the

mighty Pacific Ocean (don't spill your beer).

🍴 JED'S FOOD STORE
Café $

☎ 9365 0022; cnr Glenayr & Warners Aves, North Bondi; ☼ 6.30am-3.30pm; 🚌 381 from Bondi Junction, 380, 389; 🚹 🅥

Jed's is so relaxed, you'll feel like you're living in a uni share-house again. Reggae mellows the tattooed staff who sing and groove around; dudes sip coffee outside as kids and dogs run amok. Grab a seat for the Caribbean-style jerked potato scramble and a strong coffee.

🍴 MONGERS *Seafood* $

☎ 9365 2205; www.mongers.com.au; 42 Hall St, Bondi; ☼ noon-9pm; 🚌 381 from Bondi Junction, 380, 389; 🚹

Gourmet, grease-free fish and chips for those who are fond of tradition, but not at the expense of their waistline. Grab some low-joule grilled whiting and some thin-cut sweet-potato chips and head for the sand.

🍴 NICK'S *Mod Oz* $$$

☎ 9365 4122; www.nicksbondibeach .com.au; Bondi Pavilion, Queen Elizabeth Dr, Bondi; ☼ noon-3pm & 6-10pm; 🚌 381 from Bondi Junction, 380, 389; 🚹 🚹

This hugely popular, glass-fronted fishbowl is king of the hip Bondi

Pavilion restaurants. Mood and marketing are 'mainstream chain' (Nick's is one of five around town), but the beach views are bodacious. Try the kangaroo fillet or char-grilled octopus with tomato, fetta and olives.

🍴 NORTH BONDI ITALIAN FOOD *Italian* $$$
☎ 9300 4400; www.idrb.com; 118-20 Ramsgate Ave, North Bondi; ⏰ noon-late Wed-Sun, 6pm-late Mon & Tue; 🚌 381 from Bondi Junction, 380, 389; ♿ 🅅
Expansive windows float your eyes beyond the terrace to the sighing North Bondi swell. You won't hear any sighs inside (it's all hard surfaces and conversations) but the pasta, seafood, soups and salads engage your other senses. Try the generous wild boar *papardelle*. Wines by the glass.

🍴 SWELL *Mod Oz* $$
☎ 9386 5001; www.swellrestaurant .com.au; 465 Bronte Rd, Bronte; ⏰ 7am-10pm; 🚌 378; ♿ 🅅
Pull up a pew next to Anthony LaPaglia and/or Jennifer Hawkins for seaside Swell's spanking day-turns-to-night menu. Greet the day with poached eggs, pumpkin, feta and spinach, linger into lunch with a snazzy steak sandwich and return at dinnertime for the salt-and-pepper squid.

🍸 DRINK
🍸 BEACH ROAD HOTEL *Pub*
☎ 9130 7247; www.beachrdhotel.com .au; 71 Beach Rd, Bondi; admission free; ⏰ 10am-2.30am Mon-Fri, 9am-12.30am Sat, 10am-10pm Sun; 🚌 381 from Bondi Junction, 380, 389; ♿
Weekends at this big, yellow pub are a boisterous multilevel alcoholiday, with Bondi types (bronzed and brooding) and woozy out-of-towners playing pool, drinking beer and digging live bands and DJs. Sleep off your hangover upstairs.

🍸 COOGEE BAY HOTEL *Pub*
☎ 9665 0000; www.coogeebayhotel.com .au; cnr Coogee Bay Rd & Arden St, Coogee; admission free; ⏰ 9am-3am Thu-Sat, to midnight Sun, to 1am Mon-Wed; 🚌 353 from Bondi Junction, 372-4, 313-4; ♿
Despite a recent brown-tinged controversy, this rambling, rowdy complex still packs in the backpackers for live music, a beaut beer garden, cocktail lounge and sports bar. Sit on a stool overlooking the beach, sip a cold one and wait for the perfect set.

🍸 MOCEAN *Bar*
☎ 9300 9888; www.moceanbondi.com; Basement, 34a Campbell Pde, Bondi; admission free; ⏰ 6pm-midnight Wed-Sun; 🚌 381 from Bondi Junction, 380, 389
Sexy surfers and their suntanned girlfriends carve it up to funk and

Gerard Reinmuth
Sydney architect, director of Terroir (www.terroir.com.au)

Favourite Sydney building? The Opera House (p53) is clearly Sydney's best building, but the architect Utzon was sacked midconstruction, and he went back to Denmark. No-one quite knew what to do after the Opera House! **Public spaces?** Sydney's best spatial experiences are natural: the Bondi to Coogee Clifftop Trail (p140) and the Manly Scenic Walkway (p142). Icebergs (p128) at Bondi is a clever piece of urban design. **Does Sydney architecture detract from the landscape?** Yes. There are some extreme moments here when the building is so bad, but the environment is so good! **Are there moves towards sustainable Sydney design?** State politics and Sydney's consumerist culture make it difficult for sustainable decisions to be made: Sydney is probably Australia's least sustainable city. **Are you optimistic about Sydney's architectural future?** Yes! There are a lot of young, 'pro-house' architects here, and a new generation of sharp, enthusiastic, media-savvy designers. The next decade will see them flex some muscle.

SYDNEY ROCK POOLS

Sydneysiders aren't always desperate to hurl themselves into the Pacific. Sometimes they just want to swim a few salty laps without malicious dumpers or ocean dwellers to contend with. So inclined, they head for the protected tidal pools built below the cliffs at rocky beach-ends. From north to south, the following beaches have rock pools: Palm, Whale, Bilgola, Newport, Mona Vale, Collaroy, Dee Why, Curl Curl, Freshwater, Queenscliff, Bondi, Bronte, Coogee and Cronulla. Great for kids, they're regularly drained and scoured clean of oysters, sand and seaweed, and except for Bondi Icebergs, they're free.

R & B at this subterranean Bondi bar. The cool, moody interior makes an urbane departure from the sandy stresses of the beach.

 # PLAY

☆ BONDI OPENAIR CINEMA
Cinema

☎ 1300 438 849; www.bondiopenair .com.au; Bondi Pavilion, Queen Elizabeth Dr, Bondi; tickets $20/18; ☼ 7pm Jan & Feb; ⊕ 381 from Bondi Junction, 380, 389; ♿ ♿

The best Sydney can offer: outdoor summer cinema on a massive screen with surround-sound, beachy sunsets and swanky food and wine. In the city, **OpenAir Cinema** (☎ 1300 366 649; www.stgeorge .com.au/openair; Mrs Macquaries Pt, Royal Botanic Gardens; tickets $23/21; ☼ 6.30pm; ♿ ⊕ ⚓ Circular Quay) is the same but different. Bookings essential.

☆ DIVE CENTRE BONDI *Activity*
☎ 9369 3855; www.divebondi.com .au; 198 Bondi Rd, Bondi; courses from

$225; ☼ 8.30am-6pm Mon-Fri, 7.30am-6pm Sat & Sun; ⊕ 381 from Bondi Junction, 380, 389

With so much water around Sydney, it's tempting to see what's under the surface. This reputable company runs learn-to-dive courses and shore and boat dives for absolute beginners through to experienced submariners. Dive sites include North Bondi, Gordons Bay and South Head.

☆ LET'S GO SURFING
Activity

☎ 9365 1800; www.letsgosurfing.com .au; 128 Ramsgate Ave, North Bondi; 2hr lesson $85/75, board & wetsuit hire (no instruction) per 2hr $30; ☼ 9am-7pm; ⊕ 381 from Bondi Junction, 380, 389

Always wanted to join the rubbery tribe bobbing around in the Bondi waves? Here's your chance: two-hour, small-group lessons including board and wetsuit – paddle out the back, wait for a fat set and get radical, dude. Ask about lessons at Maroubra.

>MANLY

Laid-back Manly clings to a narrow isthmus between ocean and harbour beaches near North Head, Sydney Harbour's northern gatepost. Surrounded by stuffy harbour enclaves, Manly, with it's shaggy surfers, dusty labourers and relaxed locals, makes a refreshing change.

One of the highlights of the Manly experience is actually getting there. The ferry ride from Circular Quay (on either a bumbly, old-time ferry or slick, high-speed JetCat) takes you out towards the Heads, weaving through harbour traffic, past ritzy waterside homes and leafy patches of Sydney Harbour National Park – as good as any harbour tour for the price of a ferry ticket.

The Corso connects Manly's ocean and harbour beaches – surf shops, burger joints, juice bars and lousy cappuccino cafés proliferate. The refurbished Manly Wharf has classier cafés, pubs and restaurants, while Sydney Rd has a weekend craft market. The amazingly varied 10km Manly Scenic Walkway (p142) tracks west from Manly around the harbour.

MANLY

👁 SEE
Manly Art Gallery & Museum 1 A2
Manly Quarantine Station 2 B6
North Fort 3 C6
Oceanworld 4 A2

🛍 SHOP
100% Mambo 5 B2

🍴 EAT
Bower Restaurant 6 C3
Le Kiosk 7 D3

🍸 DRINK
Manly Wharf Hotel 8 A3

⭐ PLAY
Manly Blades 9 B2
Manly Surf School 10 B1

NEIGHBOURHOODS

MANLY

 SEE
MANLY ART GALLERY & MUSEUM
☎ 9976 1420; www.manly.nsw.gov.au /gallery.html; West Esplanade; admission free; ⏱ 10am-5pm Tue-Sun; 🚢 Manly 🚌 151, 169 E69 from Wynyard; ♿

A short stroll from Manly Wharf is this passionately managed community gallery, maintaining a local focus with exhibits of surf craft, swimwear and beachy bits-and-pieces. There's also a ceramics gallery, and lots of old Manly photos to peer at.

MANLY QUARANTINE STATION
☎ 9976 6220, tours 9977 5145; www .qstation.com.au; North Head Scenic Dr; tours from $34/22; 🚢 Manly then 🚌 135, or water taxi

The eerie Manly Quarantine Station was used to isolate newly arrived epidemic disease carriers between 1832 and 1984. Take a day tour, or rattle some skeletons on the adults-only or family ghost tours. Call ahead for the tour schedule.

NORTH FORT
☎ 9976 6102; www.northfort.org.au; North Head Scenic Dr; $11/8; ⏱ 10am-6pm Wed-Sun; 🚌 135

North Head Scenic Dr, heading south from Manly, provides stunning ocean, harbour and city views. Along the way is the Royal Australian Artillery National Museum at North Fort – tunnels, guns and history for the military-minded.

OCEANWORLD
☎ 8251 7877; www.oceanworld.com .au; West Esplanade; admission $18/13; ⏱ 10am-5.30pm, last admission

WORTH THE TRIP
A 12-minute ferry ride from Circular Quay or a short drive from Manly, **Taronga Zoo** (☎ 9969 2777; www.zoo.nsw.gov.au; Bradleys Head Rd, Mosman; admission $41/28, ZooPass incl return ferry from Circular Quay, admission & Sky Safari $39/23.50; ⏱ 9am-5pm, last admission 4.30pm; 🚢 from Circular Quay 🚌 247 from Wynyard; ♿ 🚼) has 75 hectares of bushy harbour hillside chock-full of kangaroos, koalas and similarly hirsute Australians. The zoo's 4000 critters have million-dollar harbour views but seem blissfully unaware of the privilege.

Highlights include the Sky Safari cable car, platypus habitat, Asian elephants display and the nightly **Roar & Snore** (☎ 9978 4791; tickets 132 849; tickets $216/166.50), an over-night family experience with a night-time safari, barbecue and tents under the stars. Shows and feedings happen throughout the day; there are twilight concerts in summer.

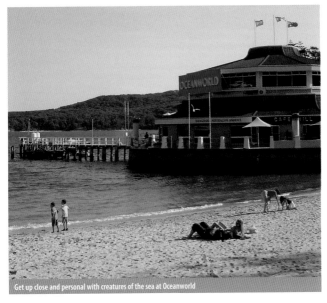
Get up close and personal with creatures of the sea at Oceanworld

4.45pm; 🔔 **Manly** 🚌 **151, 169 E69 from Wynyard**

This ain't the place to come if you're on your way to Manly Beach for a surf. Inside this daggy-looking '80s building are underwater glass tubes through which you become alarmingly intimate with 3m sharks. Reckon they're not hungry? Shark Dive Xtreme (introductory/certified $250/185) takes you into their world…

 # SHOP

100% MAMBO *Fashion*

☎ 9977 9171; www.mambo.com.au; 80 The Corso; ⏰ 10am-6pm; 🔔 Manly 🚌 151, 169 E69 from Wynyard

It's hard to go anywhere in Australia these days without copping an eyeful of Mambo's kooky, bulbous, provocative designs, emblazoned across T-shirts, baseball caps, surfboards, board-shorts and bikinis. Ugly never looked so pretty.

WORTH THE TRIP

Romantic Spanish mission–style architecture, sweeping harbour views and outstanding food collide at one of Sydney's enduringly popular restaurants, Balmoral's **Bathers' Pavilion** (☎ 9969 5050; www.batherspavilion.com.au; 4 The Esplanade, Balmoral; ☼ noon-2.30pm & 6-10.30pm; ☒ 175 then 275 from Spit Junction; ☒ ☑). It's open from 9am on Sunday. Under the same roof, Bathers' Café also opens for breakfast from 7am, serving equally scrumptious fare at more democratic prices.

🍴 EAT

🍴 BOWER RESTAURANT
Mod Oz $$

☎ /fax 9977 5451; cnr Marine Pde & Bower La; ☼ 8am-3pm; ☒ Manly ☒ 151, 169 E69 from Wynyard

Follow the path east from Manly's ocean beach to this little white food room, within sea-spray's reach of Fairy Bower Beach. The seafood-and-champagne risotto is a knockout, it's BYO and staff are not afraid to let Olivia Newton John wail from the stereo.

🍴 LE KIOSK *Mod Oz* $$$

☎ 9977 4122; www.lekiosk.com.au; 1 Marine Pde, Shelly Beach; ☼ noon-3pm daily, 6.30-9.30pm Fri-Sun; ☒ Manly ☒ 151, 169 E69 from Wynyard; ☒ ☑

'Le Kiosk' sounds ugly but defines romance – a sandstone cottage, subtle lighting, open fireplace and the lull of lapping waves. The food proves a worthy paramour; swoon over snapper fillet with sautéed calamari, bacon, chilli and cauliflower.

🍸 DRINK

🍸 MANLY WHARF HOTEL *Pub*

☎ 9977 1266; www.manlywharfhotel.com.au; Manly Wharf, East Esplanade; admission free; ☼ 11.30am-midnight Mon-Sat, 11am-10pm Sun; ☒ Manly ☒ 151, 169, E69 from Wynyard; ☒

On the harbour side of Manly, the fabulously well-designed Manly Wharf Hotel is perfect for sunny afternoon beers. Tuck away a few middys after a hard day in the surf then pour yourself onto the ferry.

⭐ PLAY

⭐ MANLY BLADES
Activity

☎ 9976 3833; www.manlyblades.com.au; 2/49 North Steyne; hire per hr with safety gear $20, lessons per hr $60; ☼ 9am-6pm; ☒ Manly ☒ 151,169 E69 from Wynyard

Work up an appetite or work off your lunch with a skate along Manly Beach promenade. These guys will get you gliding on

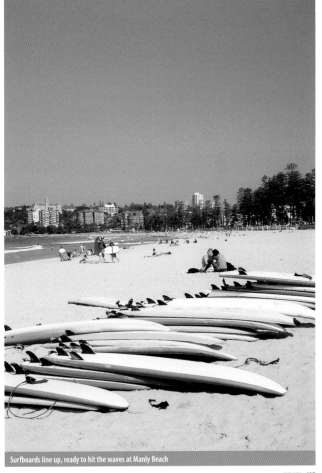

Surfboards line up, ready to hit the waves at Manly Beach

V

NEIGHBOURHOODS

MANLY

ENTER SANDMEN

Manly was one of the first places in Australia to be given a European moniker – history suggests Captain Phillip named the beach after the 'manly' physiques of the Aborigines he met on the sand here in 1788. Perpetuating this reputation today are the bronzed bodysurfing battalions in the waves. If you're feeling inadequate, head for protected Shelly Beach, east of the main beach.

top-of-the-range inline skates, skateboards and mountain bikes. Private skate lessons are available if you're less than proficient.

☆ MANLY SURF SCHOOL
Activity

☎ 9977 6977; www.manlysurfschool
.com; North Steyne Surf Club; 2hr lesson incl board & wetsuit $55/45; 🕙 9am-6pm; 🚊 Manly 🚌 151, 169 E69 from Wynyard

If Bondi isn't your scene, this outfit offers small-group surfing lessons in the Manly shore-breaks. Reformed professional surfers will have you upright on big stable surfboards before you can say, 'Dude, this green room is gnarly!' Also located at Palm Beach and Collaroy.

>WALKING TOURS

Weave your way along the Bondi to Coogee Clifftop Trail

BONDI TO COOGEE CLIFFTOP TRAIL

A quintessential Sydney encounter, this stunning coastal walk rambles south from Bondi Beach along the clifftops to Coogee via Clovelly, Tamarama and Bronte beaches, interweaving panoramic views, swimming spots and foody delights.

Start your explorations at the Eora **Aboriginal rock engravings (1)** between the tower and the cliffs at Bondi Golf Club. Some decades ago they were bizarrely 're-grooved' by the well-meaning but insensitive local council. March south along Military Rd, left into Ramsgate Ave and feel the seaspray on your skin at the **lookout (2)**. The trail then runs along the rocks to the beach – if the surf's humongous, stay high and dry on Ramsgate Ave. Dunk yourself in the surf then rummage through Sunday's funky **Bondi Markets (3**; p123), or stick your head into **Bondi Pavilion (4**; p123) for an exhibition or performance.

Grab a bite, a bikini or some surfboard wax on **Campbell Parade (5)** then promenade along the beach to Notts Ave and the glistening **Icebergs (6;** p128) pool and restaurant. Step onto the cliff path at the end of Notts Ave – the blustery sandstone cliffs and grinding Pacific Ocean couldn't be more spectacular (watch for dolphins, whales and surfers). Slide past sex-pot **Tamarama Beach (7**; p14) to **Bronte Beach (8**; p122) – take your pick of beachy cafés for a coffee, a chunky lunch or a quick snack.

Continue past the **Bronte Baths (9)** through the sun-bleached **Waverley Cemetery (10)** where writer Henry Lawson and cricketer Victor Trumper are among the subterranean dwellers. Duck into the sunbaked **Clovelly Bowling Club (11)** for a beer or a game of bowls, then breeze past the cockatoos, banksias and canoodling lovers in Burrows Park and Bundock Park to **Clovelly Beach (12)**. The concrete terrace skirting the long, skinny bay makes it more a pool than a beach, but the swell still surges in. A beloved friendly grouper fish lived here for many years until he was speared by a tourist. Bring your snorkel, but don't go killing anything.

Follow the footpath up through the car park, along Cliffbrook Pde then down the steps to the upturned dinghies lining **Gordons Bay** (**13**). The trail continues through Dunningham Reserve to **Giles Baths** (**14**), then lands you smack-bang on glorious **Coogee Beach** (**15**; p122). Swagger into the **Coogee Bay Hotel** (**16**; p129) and toast your efforts with a nice cold lager.

distance 5km **duration** Two to three hours ▶ **start** 🚌 380, 389 Circular Quay to North Bondi ● **end** 🚌 372-4, 313-4 Coogee to Circular Quay

MANLY SCENIC WALKWAY

This epic walk tracks west from Manly through rugged Sydney Harbour National Park (wear strong shoes). It's easy to forget you're right in the middle of Sydney!

Check the surf at **Manly Beach (1)** then cruise down the Corso to **Oceanworld (2**; p134) on West Esplanade. Scan the view through the Heads from **Fairlight (3)**, and the yachts tugging on their moorings near **Forty Baskets Beach (4)**. Kookaburras cackle as you enter **Sydney Harbour National Park (5)** and approach **Reef Beach (6)**. The track becomes steep, sandy and rocky further into the park – keep an eye out for wildflowers, fat goannas sunning themselves and spiders in bottlebrush trees. The views from **Dobroyd Head (7)** are unforgettable. Check out the **deserted 1930s sea shanties (8)** at the base of Crater Cove cliff, and **Aboriginal rock carvings (9)** on an unsigned ledge left of the track before the turnoff to **Grotto Point Lighthouse (10)**. Becalmed **Castle Rock Beach (11)** is at the western end of the national park.

There are no eateries en route, so eat at Manly beforehand, or picnic on **Clontarf Beach (12)**. Bus into town from the southern end of the **Spit Bridge (13)**.

distance 10km **duration** Four hours ▶ **start** ⚓ Circular Quay to Manly 🚌 151 from QVB, 169, E69 from Wynyard ● **end** 🚌 151,169, E69 from the Spit Bridge to Wynyard

SOUTH HEAD SHUFFLE

Take the Watsons Bay ferry from Circular Quay. The **Tree of Knowledge** (**1**) grew near the pier – an enormous fig where nefarious sea-dogs once convened. Fuel-up on fish and chips at **Doyles on the Beach** (**2**; p128).

Check out the restored Cove St **fishermen's cottages** (**3**), then cross Camp Cove Reserve beneath an **ancient fig** (**4**). From Camp St, turn right into Pacific St then descend the car park steps for magical **harbour views** (**5**). A **WWII antitorpedo boom** (**6**) stretched from here to the north shore.

In 1788 Governor Philip landed at **Camp Cove** (**7**). Take the steps beyond the beach past an 1872 **canon** (**8**) and gay/nude **Lady Bay** (**9**). Veer left to the 1858 **Lightkeeper's Cottage** (**10**), circumnavigating South Head for **North Head views** (**11**), the red-and-white **Hornby Light** (**12**) and South Head's original **fortifications** (**13**), defending Sydney against threats real and imagined. Backtrack through bottlebrush birdlife to Camp Cove.

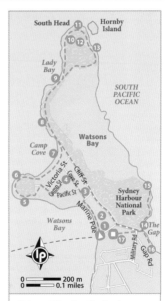

distance 2.5km **duration** Two hours
► **start** 🚢 Wharf 4, Circular Quay to Watsons Bay ● **end** 🚢 Watsons Bay to Circular Quay

Trundle along Cliff St to **The Gap** (**14**), where wedding proposals and suicides abound. The Birrabirragal people once lived at **Gap Bluff** (**15**). To the right is the **anchor of the Dunbar** (**16**), wrecked offshore in 1857.

Continue south along the clifftops, or cross **Robertson Park** (**17**) to the ferry.

>SNAPSHOTS

Sydney is a worldly, open-minded kinda town, with all sorts of people from all over the place. Shop, sleep, eat, drink and play however you want to – no-one's going to judge you! Perhaps the only rule is to at least look at a beach – they're the best in the world!

Get among the locals at Bondi Beach (p122)

SNAPSHOTS

ACCOMMODATION

You'll have no problem finding a place to lay your head in Sydney, with solid options in every price range. During the busy summer months, most hotels and hostels increase room rates and cancel promotional deals. Conversely, when tumbleweeds blow through lobbies in the slower winter months, you can often strike a bargain.

For a standard double room in a deluxe hotel, expect to pay $350 and up. For a top-end room you'll pay between $250 and $350. For a standard midranger it'll be $125 to $250, and for a budget double you'll pay up to $125 per night. Midrange to deluxe hotels publish 'rack' rates (standard rates) but it's worth ringing ahead to see if there are any current specials. Many hotels cater primarily to business travellers, so their weekend rates may be lower. Breakfast and on-site parking is sometimes included in the room price. All accommodation has a 10% goods and services tax (GST) included in the price.

Predictably, a view can play a big part in determining the price of a Sydney room. You can almost feel your wallet losing weight as you ride hotel elevators upwards to lofty suites, where Sydney's waterscapes reveal themselves from sky-high balconies. Down at the beach it's the same story – Manly, Bondi and Coogee have plenty of accommodation with surf-strewn views, but you'll be shelling out the dollars for even a glimpse. Between November and February, prices at beachside hotels can be as much as 40% higher. But what the hell, you're on holiday! Why not enjoy yourself?

If you're bunking down in budget lodgings, Sydney has plenty of hostels, heritage pubs and guesthouses. Facilities range from basic dorms to well-kept rooms with en suite, TV and shared kitchens.

 Hotels & Hostels

Need a place to stay? Find and book it at lonelyplanet .com. More than 60 properties are featured for Sydney – each personally visited, thoroughly reviewed and happily recommended by a Lonely Planet author. From hostels to high-end hotels, we've hunted out the places that will bring you unique and special experiences. Read independent reviews by authors and other travellers, and get practical information including amenities, maps and photos. Then reserve your room simply and securely via Hotels & Hostels – our online booking service. It's all at lonelyplanet.com/hotels.

Serviced apartments, which offer hotel-style convenience plus self-catering cooking facilities, can be good value, especially for families. They vary in size from hotel rooms with a bar fridge and microwave to full-blown three-bedroom apartments.

Read up on Sydney's neighbourhoods (p30) before deciding where to settle: party people should head for Kings Cross, Darlinghurst, Paddington or Bondi; shoppers, gourmands and highlight hunters should shoot for The Rocks, city centre, Darling Harbour or Chinatown. If you want to keep things a little more low-key, try Glebe, Potts Point, Surry Hills or Manly. On a short trip, don't be tempted by cheaper rates further out of town – Sydney's public transport is good, but not that good. You don't want to spend most of your time sardined into a train or bus.

WEB RESOURCES

Booking through an accommodation agency such as **Tourism NSW** (www.visitnsw.com.au) can sometimes land you a discount. Well worth checking is Lonely Planet's 'Hotels & Hostels' online accommodation review and booking service (see opposite). For tasty deals on mainstream hotels and serviced apartments try www.check-in.com.au, and of course the big-name players including www.expedia.com.au, www.lastminute.com.au and www.wotif.com.

BEST ON A BUDGET
> Hotel Altamont (www.altamont.com.au)
> Pensione Hotel (www.pensione.com.au)
> Wake Up! (www.wakeup.com.au)
> Harbour City Backpackers (www.harbourcitybackpackers.com.au)
> Manly Beach House (www.manlybeachhouse.com.au)

BEST FOR SWEET SEDUCTION
> Medusa (www.medusa.com.au)
> Observatory Hotel (www.observatoryhotel.com.au)
> Kirketon Hotel (www.kirketon.com.au)
> Hilton (www.sydney.hilton.com)
> Establishment (www.establishmenthotel.com)

BEST BANG FOR YOUR BUCK
> Vulcan Hotel (www.vulcanhotel.com.au)
> Hotel 59 (www.hotel59.com.au)
> Blacket (www.theblacket.com)
> Royal Sovereign Hotel (www.royalsov.com.au)
> Lord Nelson Brewery Hotel (www.lordnelson.com.au)

BEST BY THE BEACH
> Dive (www.divehotel.com.au)
> Ravesi's (www.ravesis.com.au)
> 101 Addison Rd (www.bb-manly.com.au)
> Sinclairs of Bondi (www.sinclairsbondi.com.au)
> Manly Pacific (www.accorhotels.com.au)

GAY & LESBIAN SYDNEY

Gay and lesbian culture is mainstream in Sydney; Oxford St around Taylor Sq is the centre of arguably the second-largest gay community in the world. Some local gays think Taylor Sq has become something of a touristy gay ghetto and have migrated to areas of Kings Cross instead. Newtown is home to the city's lesbian scene.

Of course, the highlight of the Sydney gay and lesbian calendar is the annual Mardi Gras festival (p20). Started in 1978 as a political march to commemorate New York's Stonewall riots, Mardi Gras has evolved into a month-long arts extravaganza attracting more visitors and bringing in more tourist dollars than any other event in Australia.

The festival culminates in a raucous street parade and party on the last Saturday in February. The parade – a rampant procession of up to 200 glitzy floats – begins on the corner of Elizabeth and Liverpool Sts at around 7.30pm, and prances the length of Oxford St before trundling down Flinders St, Moore Park Rd and Driver Ave to the Entertainment Quarter. If you want to be among the hundreds of thousands of folks watching the parade, find some friends with a balcony view of Oxford St or cordon off a patch of pavement several hours before it starts. Be sure to bring a milk crate to stand on (oh-so-suddenly scarce) and take some water with you. Tickets to the bacchanalian Mardi Gras Party normally sell out by mid-January and are usually only available to Mardi Gras members, though interstate and overseas visitors can get temporary membership.

The free gay press incudes *SX* and *Sydney Star Observer*. *Lesbians on the Loose* (www.lotl.com) also has extensive listings. For counselling and referral call the **Gay and Lesbian Counselling Service of NSW** (☎ 8594 9596; www .glcsnsw.org.au). **Gay and Lesbian Tourism Australia** (www.galta.com.au) has a wealth of information about gay and lesbian travel in Oz.

In New South Wales (NSW) it's legal for men to have sex with men over 18, and for women to have sex with women over 16. Despite broad acceptance, there is still a homophobic streak among some community sections and violence against homosexuals is not unknown.

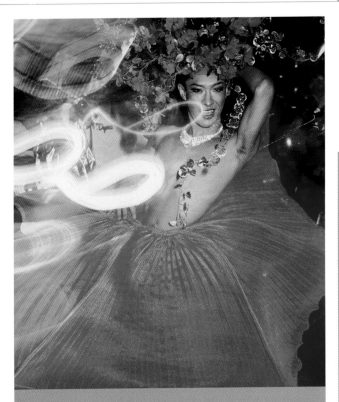

BEST GAY CLUBS
> Arq (p107)
> Phoenix, at Exchange Hotel (p107)
> Slide (p108)
> Midnight Shift (p108)
> Stonewall Hotel (p109)

BEST G & L PUBS, BARS & DRAG
> Green Park Hotel (p104)
> Oxford Hotel (p106)
> Gazebo Wine Garden (p104)
> Sydney by Diva (p109)

HEALTH & FITNESS

Sydney's sunshine, parks and unashamed vanity provide plenty of impetus to get your pulse pumping and your bod buffed. Most large hotels have a gym and swimming pool for guests; many make these facilities available to visitors for a fee. Otherwise, there's an abundance of independent gyms around town.

Feel like a run? The foreshore from Circular Quay to Woolloomooloo – through the Royal Botanic Gardens to The Domain – is well trodden. Centennial Park, Bondi and Manly beach promenades and the Bondi to Coogee Clifftop Trail (p140) pass beneath many a sweaty sneaker.

With steep hills, narrow streets and traffic, Sydney isn't exactly bicycle-friendly, although some roads do have designated cycle lanes. **Bicycle NSW** (☎ 9218 5400; www.bicyclensw.org.au) publishes *Cycling Around Sydney* detailing city routes and paths. Centennial Park is popular for pedalling – less traffic and long pathways.

It's just plain wrong to come to Sydney and not at least have a swim at the beach. Harbour beaches offer sheltered and shark-netted swimming, but nothing beats (or cures a hangover faster than) a romp in the Pacific Ocean waves. There are 100-plus public swimming pools in Sydney and many beaches have protected rock pools (p131).

If you're itching for a surf, on the South Shore get tubed at Bondi, Tamarama, Coogee, Maroubra and Bronte. On the North Shore there are a dozen gnarly surf beaches between Manly and Palm Beach. Surfboards, boogie-boards and wetsuits can be hired from seaside shops. For lessons in how to carve up the swell, see Bondi's Let's Go Surfing (p131) and Manly Surf School (p138).

Yoga is so popular here you'd think all of Sydney was looking through its third eye. Bondi Junction is yoga central, with around 10 schools, most teaching both Hatha and Ashtanga yoga. Newtown also has several schools. Check out www.findyoga.com.au to find the nearest school to you.

Sydney's sailing schools are many; a sailing lesson (p75) is a superb way to see the harbour. The **Cruising Yacht Club of Australia** (☎ 8292 7800; www.cyca.com.au) fields general inquiries.

There are hundreds of public tennis courts in Sydney. **Tennis NSW** (☎ 1800 153 040; www.tennisnsw.com.au) lobs up information.

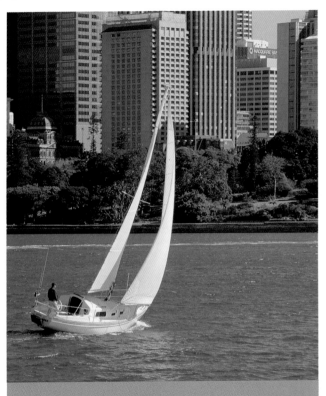

BEST SWIMMING BEACHES
> Camp Cove (p15)
> Shark Bay (p15)
> Clovelly (p140)
> Balmoral (p15)
> Between the flags at Bondi (p122)

BEST SURF BEACHES
> Bronte (p122)
> Tamarama (p14)
> Manly (p132)
> Maroubra (p14)
> Avalon (p15)

SYDNEY CUISINE

Other Australian cities hate to admit it, but Sydney – with its multicultural melting pot, abundant fresh produce and geographic assets – has won the food trifecta. Adelaide may have the great wines, Melbourne the café culture and Hobart the seafood, but Sydney has it all, and right on Sydney Harbour.

Restaurants hum, and as inner-city gentrification continues, more and more corner pubs are transforming into brasseries, bookshops are installing espresso machines and locals are finding their own kitchens increasingly wearisome.

Modern Australian cuisine – Mod Oz – continues to evolve as chefs consult Asia for fusion ingredients and Europe for technique. Cooking focuses on fresh, healthy eating, drawing on rich and diverse migrant-community influences. At the top end, celebrity chefs plate up mini-masterpieces for wealthy corporate crowds. Those on tighter budgets need not despair; thousands of cafés, bistros and restaurants offer innovative, quality meals at moderate prices.

Most of Sydney's licensed restaurants can't serve patrons alcohol unless they order a meal. Many restaurants have a good wine list, pushing Australian product. Restaurant prices are more expensive than in bottle shops – a decent drop will set you back about $30 and up. Wine sold by the glass is also widely available. Many Sydney restaurants advertise themselves as BYO. This means you can 'Bring Your Own' alcohol, though you'll generally be charged a corkage fee (anywhere from $5 to $15 per bottle, sometimes per person). Some licensed places also allow you to BYO, often restricted to bottled wine only. Smoking is banned in all restaurants, cafes, pubs and bars.

Cafés and restaurants are generally open seven days, with many cafés serving food from 7am to 10pm. Most restaurants are open for lunch and dinner, closing typically between 3pm and 6pm, while cafés and patisseries are the best bet for breakfast. Bookings are required at the more expensive restaurants, especially for dinner.

A 10% tip is customary for good restaurant service in Sydney, but feel free to vary the amount depending on your satisfaction.

BEST CLASSY BUSINESS EATS
> Aria (p55)
> Forty One (p42)
> Prime (p43)
> Bécasse (p42)
> Bistro Moncur (p118)

MOST TO-DIE-FOR VIEWS
> North Bondi Italian Food (p129)
> Altitude (p55)
> Icebergs (p128)
> Barzura (p126)
> Aqua Dining (boxed text, p55)

BEST VEGETARIAN
> Bodhi (p42)
> Green Gourmet (p83)
> Mother Chu's Vegetarian Kitchen (p43)
> Zaaffran (p73)
> Chinta Ria, Temple of Love (p72)

BEST SEAFOOD
> Boathouse on Blackwattle Bay (p81)
> Fish Face (p102)
> Mongers (p128)
> Doyles on the Beach (boxed text, p128)
> Bungalow 8 (p71)

Opposite Seafood is prepared with love at the Boathouse (p81) on Blackwattle Bay **Above** Icebergs enjoys a sweeping view (p128)

DRINKING

Pubs play a crucial role in Sydney's social scene, ranging from traditional, elaborate 19th-century affairs with pressed tin ceilings, to cavernous, tiled Art Deco masterpieces and mod, minimalist booze rooms. Bars are the domain of Sydney's urbane drinkers, and often have a dress code (oh-so-smart casual).

There are some rambling old pubs in The Rocks, but determining just how old they are is an inexact science. For sassier surrounds and long cocktail lists, join the after-work booze hounds in the city centre and around Circular Quay.

Twenty-four-hour party people head for Darlinghurst and Kings Cross – the trashy main drag, Darlinghurst Rd, has plenty of drinking (and stripping) options, though there are some stylish speakeasies around here too. Glitzy fashionistas populate Paddington's pubs; students and artists drink in Surry Hills. The inner west is great for a low-key schooner – Balmain, Glebe and Newtown have plenty of decent boozers.

Admission to most bars and pubs is free; check www.sydneypubguide .net and www.sydneycafes.com.au/bars.html for listings.

Sydney's coffee drinkers are increasingly choosy about where and how they sip their coffee. Caffeine strips include Darlinghurst Rd and Victoria St in Darlinghurst, King St in Newtown and Glebe Point Rd in Glebe.

BEST LOCAL PUBS
> Cricketers Arms Hotel (p94)
> Australian Hotel (p58)
> London Hotel (boxed text, p85)
> Green Park Hotel (p104)
> Lord Nelson Brewery Hotel (p59)

BEST DESIGNER DRINKING DENS
> Ruby Rabbit (p106)
> Zeta (p45)
> Victoria Room (p106)
> Opera Bar (p59)
> Jimmy Lik's (p105)

BEST BREW WITH A VIEW
> Bondi Social (p126)
> Blu Horizon (p58)
> Orbit Lounge Bar (p44)
> The Loft (p74)
> Manly Wharf Hotel (p136)

BEST COFFEE SHOPS
> Campos (p81)
> Bar Coluzzi (p102)
> Old Fish Shop Café (p83)
> Badde Manors (p81)
> Ampersand Café & Bookstore (p118)

GALLERY SCENE

Galleries are pivotal in Sydney's visual arts scene, fostering a tense, competitive vibe between them, particularly between the Paddington/Woollahra galleries and their Surry Hills/Redfern competitors. See the Metro section in Friday's *Sydney Morning Herald* and the monthly *Art Almanac* magazine for listings. Many galleries close through Christmas/January and on Mondays; most of them are free.

Over the past 25 years, Australian indigenous art has soared to global heights, a lofty position cemented with the opening of the Musee du quai Branly in Paris in mid-2006. The museum's façade, walls and ceilings have been gloriously painted by Aboriginal artists. Traditional methods and spiritual significance are fastidiously maintained in Aboriginal art, often finding a counterpart in Western materials – the results can be wildly original interpretations of traditional stories and ceremonial designs. Most traditional and contemporary indigenous art available in Sydney's galleries and shops comes from elsewhere in Australia, costing anywhere from $20 to $10,000.

Sydney's city centre and The Rocks are full of cheap-and-nasty tourist shops hocking varnished boomerangs and mass-produced didgeridoos, shimmering under fluoro lights. Avoid them. To ensure you make an informed, authentic purchase and don't perpetuate the nonindigenous cash-in on Aboriginal art's popularity, buy from an authentic dealer selling original art, and if the gallery doesn't pay their artists up-front, ask exactly how much of your money will make it back to the artist or community. Another good test is to request some biographical info on the artists – if the gallery can't produce it, keep walking.

BEST SMALL GALLERIES
> Object Gallery (p90)
> Iain Dawson Gallery (p112)
> Watters Gallery (p37)
> Australian Centre for Photography (p112)
> SH Ervin Gallery (p51)

BEST INDIGENOUS GALLERIES
> Yiribana Gallery, Art Gallery of NSW (p34)
> Hogarth Galleries (p112)
> Artery (p97)
> Original & Authentic Aboriginal Art (p51)
> Gannon House (p50)

PARKS, WILDLIFE & THE GREAT OUTDOORS

When the galleries, shops and restaurants start to close in, Sydney offers a smorgasbord of outdoorsy possibilities – the sun is shining, the beaches are spacey, and parks are leafy retreats.

If you're hankering for some greenery in the city, head to Hyde Park (Map p33, B4), the city centre's best lunchtime picnic spot; The Domain (Map p33, D4); or Dawes Point Park (Map p49, D1) under the Sydney Harbour Bridge. Paddington's Centennial Park (Map p111, E4) and Jubilee Park (Map p77, B2) at the end of Glebe Point Rd have boundless space.

Want some fauna with your flora? There are great zoos, aquariums and wildlife parks not far from the city centre, or you can head further out. In the western suburbs, **Featherdale Wildlife Park** (☎ 9622 1644; www.featherdale.com.au) at Doonside houses 2000 native Australians eating, sleeping, shagging and generally being beastly. **Koala Park Sanctuary** (☎ 9484 3141; www.koalapark.com) at West Pennant Hills in the north is a 4.5-hectare sanctuary with koalas, kangaroos, wombats, echidnas, dingoes and native birds. **Waratah Park Earth Sanctuary** (☎ 9986 1788; www.waratahpark.com.au) at Duffys Forest in the north was where iconic '60s Australian TV show *Skippy the Bush Kangaroo* was filmed. It's now a free-range park for kangaroos, bandicoots and potoroos.

Broke? Take your book to the beach. If you're worried about getting your gear off, don't be. Victorian conservatism banned daylight bathing in Sydney until 1903. In 1907, a new law permitted neck-to-knee swimming costumes only. By 1930, hems were on the rise – soon nude was rude no more. These days, Sydney's beaches seethe with as much skin as sand.

See also Walking Tours (p139).

BEST WILDLIFE PARKS
> Taronga Zoo (boxed text, p134)
> Sydney WildlifeWorld (p69)
> Sydney Aquarium (p68)
> Waratah Park Earth Sanctuary (above)
> Featherdale Wildlife Park (above)

BEST PLACES TO CHILL-OUT ON THE GRASS
> Royal Botanic Gardens (p35)
> Observatory Park (p52)
> Jubilee Park (above)
> Centennial Park (above)
> Hyde Park (above)

SHOPPING & MARKETS

Sydney's brash, ingrained commercial culture goes a long way towards explaining its citizens' passion for shopping. Most locals treat it as recreational activity rather than a necessity, evidenced by the teeming, cash-flapping masses at the city's numerous weekend markets. You can buy everything from gumboots to g-strings in Sydney's shops, but some of the more interesting stuff is in the galleries – Aboriginal art (p155) and cutting-edge crafts in particular.

Shopping in central Sydney can be fun, but hectic. The city centre brims with department stores, boutiques, duty-free shops and outdoor stores – shopping here is as fast and furious as Australia gets. Much more chilled-out are suburban shopping strips such as Oxford St, Paddington, Glebe Point Rd, Glebe, and King St, Newtown – long, sinuous swathes of boutiques, cafés and bookshops. Queen St, Woollahra, is antique-central.

All stores accept major credit cards. If a store accepts travellers cheques, some valid ID – a driving licence or passport – will probably be required as well. A 10% federal Goods and Services Tax (GST) is automatically included in the price of most things you buy. Visitors to Australia are entitled to a refund of any GST paid on items over $300 from one supplier; see p170 for details.

Bargaining and haggling isn't really part of Australian consumer culture – locals tend to think it's somehow undignified and shop around for the best prices instead – but it may work for you at duty-free stores and markets. Most larger stores will arrange shipment or mailing of bulky or fragile items.

BEST WEEKEND MARKETS
> Glebe Market (p78)
> Paddington Market (p116)
> Bondi Markets (p123)
> Balmain Market (boxed text, p78)
> Paddy's Markets (p70)

BEST FROCK SHOPS
> Wheels & Doll Baby (p100)
> Leona Edmiston (p116)
> Capital L (p100)
> Collette Dinnigan (p114)
> Alannah Hill (p41)

V

SPECTATOR SPORTS

Sydney loves to watch. Basketball, cricket, football, soccer, rugby, surf lifesaving, tennis and yachting draw crowds of onlookers, keen to glimpse the hard-bodied participants and their silky skills.

Sydney's National Basketball League men's team recently folded, but from October to February the Sydney Flames play in the **Women's National Basketball League** (WNBL; www.wnbl.com.au).

From October to March, Paddington's Sydney Cricket Ground (SCG) hosts interstate Sheffield Shield and international Test, World Series one-day and 20/20 cricket matches; see www.cricinfo.com.

The **Australian Football League** (AFL; www.afl.com.au) is unique, skilful and awe-inspiring. From March to September, the Sydney Swans glide across the Sydney Cricket Ground and ANZ Stadium at Homebush.

Soccer is gaining fans, thanks to the World Cup successes of the Australian Socceroos. Sydney FC play in the national **A-League** (www.a-league.com.au).

Sydney *adores* winter's **National Rugby League** (NRL; www.nrl.com.au) comp, transpiring at stadia including Paddington's Sydney Football Stadium. NSW and Queensland collide annually in the State of Origin series. The Australian Wallabies **rugby union** (www.rugbyunion.com.au) team plays internationals in Sydney periodically.

Australian icons, surf lifesavers compete at summer surf carnivals on Sydney's beaches. Contact **Surf Life Saving NSW** (☎ 9300 4000; www.slsa.asn.au).

January's Adidas International tennis tournament happens at the Sydney International Tennis Centre at Homebush; contact **Tennis NSW** (☎ 1800 153 040; www.tennisnsw.com.au).

The 18ft (5.5m) skiff yacht racing season runs from September to March. The **Sydney Flying Squadron** (☎ 9955 8350; www.sydneyflyingsquadron.com.au) conducts viewings. On Boxing Day (26 December) Sydney Harbour hosts the start of the harrowing Sydney to Hobart Yacht Race (p22).

>BACKGROUND

The complexities of Aboriginal culture are at last being recognised

BACKGROUND
HISTORY

Australia can seem to be a long way from anywhere in particular – this isolation made it the last great landmass to be 'discovered' by Europeans. But before Sydney Harbour saw its first billow of British sail, indigenous people inhabited the continent for more than 50,000 years, the world's longest continuous cultural history.

ABORIGINAL ORIGINS

When the British first sailed into Warran (the Aboriginal name for Sydney Harbour) there were an estimated 3000 Aborigines living in the area, and around one million across the continent. The Sydney region is the ancestral home of the Eora people (the Ku-ring-gai, Birrabirragal and Cadi tribes) who possessed an intimate understanding of environmental sustainability, spoke three distinct languages and maintained sophisticated sacred and artistic cultures.

Under colonial rule, Aborigines were stripped of legal rights to their land. In a typically ugly pattern of European colonisation, they were systematically incarcerated, killed or driven away by force; many more succumbed to European diseases.

A legacy of 2000 Aboriginal rock engravings exists in the Sydney area, and many Sydney suburbs have Aboriginal names.

EUROPEAN SETTLEMENT

Portuguese navigators first bumped into Australia in the 16th century, followed by Dutch explorers and the enterprising Englishman (read: pirate) William Dampier. British hunger for new world territory landed Captain James Cook on the east coast in 1770. Cook claimed the continent for England and, in a fit of creative genius, named it New South Wales (NSW).

Sailing home, Joseph Banks (Cook's naturalist) suggested relieving Britain's overcrowded prisons by transporting convicts to the new colony. The British government sparked at the concept – faraway convicts were good convicts.

In 1787 the First Fleet set sail from Portsmouth with 759 convicts aboard. At the helm was Captain Arthur Phillip, deigned to become first governor of NSW. Phillip made landfall at Botany Bay on 26 January 1788

BENNELONG

The volatile, puzzled relations between Bennelong, an Eora Aborigine, and the British are emblematic of much early contact.

In 1789 Governor Phillip kidnapped Bennelong to act as an interpreter and go-between. He initially enjoyed life at Government House, but the following years became a confused parade of escape, recapture, anger and misunderstanding. Bennelong travelled with Phillip to England, returning to Australia after two uncomfortable years and retreating from white contact.

Bennelong Point, where a house was built for him and where the Sydney Opera House now stands, bears his name.

before shunting north to Sydney Cove. He flirted with the name 'Albion' but astutely opted for Sydney (the British Home Secretary, Baron Sydney of Chislehurst, was responsible for the colonies at the time).

COLONIAL EXPANSION

In 1800 there were only three small settlements in the colony: Sydney Cove, Parramatta, and on Norfolk Island, adrift in the Pacific 1500km east of Sydney. The continent's vast interior was largely unknown. Over the next 40 years, Sydney bumbled through near-starvation and rum-fuelled political turmoil, while exploration opened up western NSW to settlers. Sydney town grew steadily, with convict transportation continuing until 1840. Free settlers arrived too, but things didn't boom until the 1850s gold rush put a rocket under the economy. Hefty discoveries near Bathurst and in Victoria had prospectors flooding in from Europe, Asia and North America. Sydney's population doubled in a decade.

THE 20TH CENTURY

On 1 January 1901 NSW became a state of the new Australian nation.

Through WWI and the Great Depression, Australia remained culturally and economically tied to Britain, but after the US defended Australia from the Japanese in WWII, a fraternal shift towards America occurred.

Postwar immigrants from the UK, Ireland and the Mediterranean brought spirit and prosperity to Australia in the 1950s and '60s and Sydney's urban area spread like spilt honey.

The face of Sydney changed again during the Vietnam War, when American GIs swarmed to the city on 'Rest and Recreation'. Kings Cross excelled in providing the kind of belt-level R&R that the troops lusted for.

WORST OF SYDNEY

Some things about Sydney can really get on your goat:

> Wheezy air, aircraft cacophony and harbour pollution
> Attitude – big fish, small pond
> Tacky Australiana shops and colonial cash-ins
> Sunburn – the southern sun bites like a shark
> Party, party, party… Don't you people read books?
> Dangerous rips at the beach – swim between the flags!
> Cockroaches – things that go crunch in the night

The bullish world economy of the 1980s sprouted a forest of bombastic new Sydney skyscrapers, with 1988's controversial celebration of the bicentenary of the British landing ruffling indigenous and pro-republican feathers.

SYDNEY TODAY

An expansive metropolis of more than four million folks, Sydney's streets buzz with business conducted in dozens of accents and tongues. Hosting the 2000 Olympic Games thrust Sydney into the global limelight, and the city wasn't shy about stepping onto the stage, the flawless success of the Games infusing confidence and pride. The Olympic ebullience is ancient history, but confidence remains.

Simmering racial tensions exploded into mob violence on Sydney's southern beaches in late 2005 – an ugly development that remains unresolvedly snagged in the city's social conscience.

LIFE AS A SYDNEYSIDER

Sydney is irresistibly multicultural, with a quarter of Sydneysiders born overseas. Before WWII Sydney was predominantly Anglo-Irish, but large postwar migrations from Italy, Greece, Yugoslavia, Lebanon and Turkey enriched the mix. The Chinese first arrived during the 1850s gold rush; Asian migration continued with large numbers of Vietnamese after the Vietnam War. Significant numbers have recently arrived from New Zealand, Thailand, Cambodia and the Philippines. Australians cherish their 'outcasts and immigrants' self-image, and despite some racial tensions, Sydneysiders remain generally tolerant of different religions and backgrounds.

A waning majority of Australians are Christian. The Presbyterian, Methodist and Congregational Union churches merged to form the Uniting Church in 1977, although the Anglican Church remains separate. Australia's Irish and Mediterranean heritage keeps Roman Catholic pews warm. Non-Christian minorities abound – Islam is Australia's second-largest religion, Jewish numbers are steady and Buddhism is increasingly popular. Around 13% of Australians claim agnosticism.

ABORIGINAL SOCIETY

Although nonindigenous Australia is at last recognising the complexities of Aboriginal culture, many are still intolerant of urban Aborigines. Aborigines comprise just 0.6% of Sydney's population, but they're marginalised and often cast as social miscreants. Misunderstandings are common, with constructive solutions to indigenous poverty, criminality and health problems placed in the 'too hard' basket. Inner-city Redfern has a large Koori (indigenous southeastern Australian) population, but the suburb's dilapidated heritage houses are fast being consumed by developers.

ETIQUETTE

The Sydney attitude can be aggressive and in-your-face, but locals are usually friendly and open-minded. Gay and lesbian Sydney is riotously uninhibited. Restaurants and sporting arenas are smoke-free. Mobile phone etiquette is forgiving, but turn yours off during meetings, movies and concerts.

Business conduct is straightforward – astute candour will seal the deal; obsequious smooth-talking (aka 'brown nosing') won't. Much business discussion happens after work at the pub – 'a couple of quieties' (a beer or two) often involves more than just a drink. Business dress is sharp with an allowance for individuality.

BIG 'UNS

Sydney currently has eight buildings over 200m tall, but as most men will assert, how big something is depends on where you measure it from: a spire can add 80m of height; an antenna even more.

By any measure, the 305m **Sydney Tower** (p36) is king of the city centre. **Chifley Tower** (2 Chifley Sq) is the highest office block, its spire scraping 244m, but the antenna on **Governor Phillip Tower** (cnr Phillip, Young & Bent Sts) spikes up to 254m. At 230m, **World Tower** (91 Liverpool St) has the highest roof.

THE ARTS

Sun, sand, surf and sin are misleading folly – Sydney is no artistic backwater. The city can't rival New York or London for artistic quantity, but Sydney breeds similarly bold and adventurous artistic attitudes. Opening nights, readings and screenings are firmly entrenched in the social calendar.

ARCHITECTURE

Sydney is predominantly a Victorian city, with much of the city's expensive inner-city housing dating from this era. Colonial structures surviving Sydney's wholesale 20th-century development are scarce, but remnants are culturally celebrated. Classy Art Deco design reigned between the two world wars, most obviously (and perhaps incongruously) in Sydney pub architecture. Some unbelievable eyesores sprouted with the lifting of the 45m building height limit in the late 1950s, with many architects accused of lazily dominating Sydney's splendorous natural setting rather than designing anything of objective or complementary beauty. Jørn Utzon's Sydney Opera House stands as a beacon of architectural delight as the city centre continues its rise.

DANCE

Dance and Sydney's body-focused audiences go hand-in-hand (and cheek-to-cheek). Australian dancers have a fearless reputation for awesome physical displays (and sometimes a lack of costume). The talented Australian Ballet troupe tours a mixed programme of classical and modern ballets, frocking-up four times a year at the Sydney Opera House.

The effervescent Sydney Dance Company (p61) leads Australia in contemporary dance. The acclaimed Bangarra Dance Theatre (p59) conjures up an incendiary blend of 50,000 years of indigenous performance tradition and vigorous new choreography.

FILM

Sydney's film industry boomed in the 1990s but things have tailed off recently, with the government failing to support the film industry with financial incentives. The best 1990s efforts, such as *Strictly Ballroom*, *Shine*, *Muriel's Wedding* and *Priscilla – Queen of the Desert,* consolidated Sydney's reputation as a top-shelf production location, while local actors such as Russell Crowe, Nicole Kidman, Naomi Watts, Cate Blanchett and Geoffrey Rush rode the Hollywood fame train.

SYDNEY ON THE SILVER SCREEN

Sydney sure is a good-lookin' sheila (see Language, p177), a fact not overlooked in these Sydney movies:

> *Two Hands* (1999; director Gregor Jordan) – vicious humour in Sydney's criminal underworld.
> *Looking for Alibrandi* (2000; director Kate Woods) – growing up Italian in Sydney suburbia.
> *Lantana* (2001; director Ray Lawrence) – mystery for grown-ups; a meditation on love, truth and grief.
> *Candy* (2006; director Neil Armfield) – Heath Ledger and Abbie Cornish in drug demise; the film adaptation of Luke Davies' 1998 grunge novel.
> *Bra Boys* (2007; director Sunny Abberton) – Maroubra's bad-boys in stark profile; narrated by the dulcet Russell Crowe.

Sydney's multimillion-dollar Fox Studios has rolled out big-budget world extravaganzas including the *Matrix* trilogy, *Mission Impossible 2*, the *Star Wars* prequels and Sydneysider Baz Luhrmann's *Moulin Rouge*.

Sydney has two international film festivals: Tropfest (p21) and Bondi's Flickerfest (p20).

MUSIC

Wrap your ears around Sydney's sounds: world-class opera, grungy pub bands, funky electronic acts. Local musos gig at pubs and clubs around the city, while international acts rock big venues such as the Sydney Entertainment Centre (p75) and the Enmore Theatre (p86).

Sydney's raucous rock scene (the Easybeats, Midnight Oil, Silverchair etc) ailed under '90s noise and licensing restrictions, but is enjoying a rockin' revival. There's an effervescent dance-music scene, with clubs and dance parties catering to every subgenre. Jazz and blues kick out the jams in venues such as the Basement (jazz; p63) and pubs such as the Empire (blues; p86).

Opera Australia wails through 18 operas a year, based (appropriately) at the Sydney Opera House (p10). The Sydney Symphony, Australia's biggest orchestra, plays 140 concerts annually, frequently at the Opera House and City Recital Hall (p45).

January's Sydney Festival (p20) tunes Sydney's diverse musical movements. The Sydney Discography (p166) lists some sound Sydney sounds.

SYDNEY DISCOGRAPHY

> *Gossip* (Paul Kelly) – 'Incident on South Dowling', 'Randwick Bells' are ringing, and 'Darlin' It Hurts' to see you down in Darlinghurst tonight.
> *Harry's Café de Wheels* (Peter Blakeley) – The only album ever named after a pie cart. Don't bother listening to it though.
> *Hourly, Daily* (You Am I) – Recorded in Sydney and oozing suburban midafternoon sensibility.
> *Love this City* (The Whitlams) – The band's named after Australia's grooviest prime minister, Gough Whitlam; the album digs into Sydney's best and worst.
> *10, 9, 8…* (Midnight Oil) – '*Sydney, nights are warm, daytime telly, blue rinse dawn…*'

LITERATURE

Sydney's literary lineage dates back to the late 1800s, when local writers including Henry Lawson, AB 'Banjo' Patterson and Miles Franklin spiked a vernacular vein. Modern Australian authors such as Patrick White (Nobel Prize 1973), Tom Keneally (Booker Prize 1982) and Peter Carey (Booker Prize 1988 and 2001) all spent time in Sydney, and have redefined what being Australian is. Keep an eye out for books by Robert Drewe, Helen Garner, David Malouf, Kate Grenville, Janette Turner Hospital, Thea Astley, Eleanor Dark, Drusilla Modjeska and Amanda Lohrey, all of whom have lived in or dedicated their pages to Sydney.

The vibrant Sydney literary scene peaks every year with the Sydney Writers Festival (p21). See www.austlit.edu.au and for more info.

PAINTING

Like Australian writers prior to the 1880s, Australian painters applied European stylings to the Antipodean condition, failing to capture Australia's bleached light, ragged forests and earthy colours with any certainty. Melbourne's distinctly Australian Heidelberg School changed this in 1885. Tom Roberts and Arthur Streeton brought the Heidelberg techniques to Sydney in 1891.

Expressionists of the 1940s such as Sidney Nolan and Arthur Boyd blazed their way to prominence and rattled the national psyche. Sydney's Brett Whiteley (1939–92) was an internationally notorious *enfant terrible* who let loose with luscious, colourful, orgasmic canvases. His Surry Hills studio is preserved as an interactive art gallery (p90).

ABORIGINAL ART

Art is integral to Aboriginal culture, a conduit between past and present, supernatural and earthly, people and land. Aboriginal art is immersed in 'The Dreaming' – a vast unchanging network of life and land tracing back to spiritual ancestors.

Aboriginal art gained broad cross-cultural exposure in the 1980s and '90s when galleries discovered its virtue and value. Dot paintings are exquisite, as are Tiwi Island woodcarvings and fabrics, Arnhem Land bark paintings and central Australian prints. Many Sydney galleries specialise in Aboriginal and Torres Strait Islander art. See p155 for some tips on how to responsibly approach an indigenous art purchase.

THEATRE

Sydney's theatrical tastes can seem stuck in a 1970s holding pattern – mainstream blockbuster musicals and crowd-friendly productions are the norm, but some small companies stage more experimental works. Australia's geographic isolation and sense of 'cultural cringe' means that truly local productions are rare, and not particularly well paid. Actors tend to migrate towards film and TV, or crack the boards overseas.

Sydney's most successful theatre company is the Sydney Theatre Company (p63). The National Institute of Dramatic Art (NIDA) is a breeding ground for new talent – Cate Blanchett, Judy Davis, Mel Gibson and Hugo Weaving are all graduates. Smaller theatre companies

BOOKISH SYDNEY

Browse the bookshelves for a Sydney-centric read:
> *The Harp in the South* and *Poor Man's Orange*, Ruth Park (1948 & 1949) – impoverished Surry Hills family life
> *Voss*, Patrick White (1957) – the unforgiving outback versus Sydney's colonial life
> *Unreliable Memoirs*, Clive James (1980) – boy-Clive in Sydney's southern 'burbs
> *The Bodysurfers*, Robert Drewe (1983) – seductive stories from the Northern Beaches
> *Lilian's Story*, Kate Grenville (1985) – the life of Sydney eccentric Bea Miles
> *The Last Magician*, Janette Turner Hospital (1992) – seedy corruption around Newtown Station
> *He Died with a Felafel in His Hand*, John Birmingham (1994) – beer, bongs and cockroaches
> *The Cross*, Mandy Sayer (1995) – sleazy '70s Kings Cross murder
> *30 Days in Sydney*, Peter Carey (2001) – tales from behind the Venetian blinds
> *Safety*, Tegan Bennet (2006) – truth and frailty on the banks of the Parramatta River

such as Griffin at the Stables Theatre (p109), Company B (p95) and the Darlinghurst Theatre Company (p107) are producing exciting work.

Notable stage actors include Angie Millikin, Jackie Weaver, Marcus Graham and John Howard (no, not the former prime minister). Directors of note include John Bell, Neil Armfield, Adam Cook and Lindy Davies.

ENVIRONMENT

Sydney and its stupendous harbour are encircled by parks and forests. Beauty comes naturally, as does the incentive to keep things looking good. Locals generate as much mess as anyone, but they're also environmentally aware.

Sydney's Gods of Rain don't pull any punches, with summer downpours sending people scurrying. Historically, Sydney's harbour and beaches gasped and clogged after heavy rains, but million-dollar litter traps now prevent a lot of rubbish flowing into the harbour. Still, swimming at harbour beaches such as Balmoral or Seven Shillings after a big storm can be a soupy experience.

Airport noise creates headaches under the flight path – the government has tried to calm underslept locals by spreading aircraft trajectories.

The air in the city and eastern suburbs is generally clean and breezy; the west can get wheezy.

GOVERNMENT & POLITICS

Sydney is the capital of NSW and seat of state government, which holds court in Parliament House on Macquarie St.

NSW has two main political parties: the left-wing Australian Labor Party and right-wing Liberal/National party coalition. At the time of writing, Labor was in power, with new premier Nathan Rees at the wheel.

A WHALE OF A TIME

Apocalyptic commercial whaling in the 19th century drove them away, but whales have recently returned to Sydney Harbour. A traditional detour for whales migrating south for the summer, the harbour has hosted pods of humpback and southern right whales breaching below the Harbour Bridge regularly over the past five years. If you're lucky enough to be out on the water with them (p63), give them a wide berth – they're bigger than you are, and humanity owes them a little peace and quiet.

Members of the Australian Greens, Australian Democrats and several independents also populate Parliament.

Sydneysiders can be wryly cynical about state politics. State elections run every four years, with the Labor Party currently in the political driver's seat. Despite Labor's comfortable majority, some left-leaning Sydneysiders feel the party has abandoned traditional values to court big-business dollars. Your views on Australia's prospective move towards becoming a republic may see you lauded as a visionary, or tarred, feathered and banished to the Blue Mountains.

Don't expect much saucy media coverage of politicians' sex lives. Perhaps it's an aesthetic damnation, but locals don't drool over Clinton-Lewinsky/Tory-sex-romp scandals. A contraceptive distance is maintained between the media and politicians.

ECONOMY

Sydney is Australia's chief commercial, financial and industrial centre, whipping up a quarter of Australia's economic activity. As a financial centre, Sydney houses 'the big three' – the Reserve Bank of Australia, Australian Stock Exchange and Sydney Futures Exchange – and most of Australia's major banks have their head offices in Sydney. It's also a transport epicentre, with two harbours – Port Jackson (Sydney Harbour) and Botany Bay – a hyperactive airport and a spider-web rail network. The majority of Australia's foreign trade flows through Sydney and NSW. Despite all this, Sydney hasn't been immune from the global financial meltdown, with its growth rate recently nudging below the national average – NSW premier Nathan Rees is feeling the heat!

Sydney tourism is coming down from a boom period, but still employs one in 12 workers. Brisbane and Cairns have taken a slice of Sydney's tourist pie, but expect Sydney to handle your arrival with aplomb.

DIRECTORY
TRANSPORT
ARRIVAL & DEPARTURE
AIR

Sydney's major airport is **Kingsford Smith airport** (☎ 9667 9111; www .sydneyairport.com.au), 10km south of the city centre. The T1 (international) and T2 and T3 (domestic) terminals are a 4km, $5.50 bus or train ride apart. Getting to the city from Kingsford Smith (or vice versa) is easiest by train or car. To confirm arrival/departure times, call airlines directly or log on to the airport website's 'Flight Search'.

BUS

Interstate and regional bus travellers arrive at **Sydney Coach Terminal** (☎ 9281 9366; fax 9281 0123; cnr Eddy Ave & Pitt St; ☼ 6am-10.30pm), outside Central station. The major bus companies have offices nearby.

TRAIN

Sydney's main rail terminus for Countrylink interstate and regional services is **Central station** (☎ 13 22 32; www.countrylink.info; Eddy Ave). Staffed ticket booths are open 6am to 10pm; ticket machines operate 24 hours. Call for information, arrival and departure times and reservations.

VISA

Visas are required for all overseas visitors except New Zealand nationals who sheepishly receive a 'special category' visa on arrival. Visa application forms are available from diplomatic missions, travel agents, the **Department of Immigration and Citizenship** (☎ 13 18 81; www.immi .gov.au), or visit the **Australian Electronic Travel Authority** (www.eta.immi.gov.au).

CUSTOMS, DUTY FREE & TAX REFUNDS

Cash amounts of more than A$10,000 and goods of animal or

CLIMATE CHANGE & TRAVEL

Travel – especially air travel – is a significant contributor to global climate change. At Lonely Planet, we believe that all travellers have a responsibility to limit their personal impact. As a result, we have teamed with Rough Guides and other concerned industry partners to support Climate Care, which allows travellers to offset the greenhouse gases they are responsible for with contributions to energy-saving projects and other climate-friendly initiatives in the developing world. Lonely Planet offsets all staff and author travel. For more information, turn to the responsible travel pages on www.lonelyplanet.com. For details on offsetting your carbon emissions and a carbon calculator, go to www.climatecare.org.

TRAVEL TO/FROM THE AIRPORT

	Taxi	Train	Bus: Sydney Airporter	Bus: Manly Airport Bus
Pick-up point	outside domestic & international terminals	below domestic & international terminals	outside domestic & international terminals	outside domestic & international terminals
Drop-off point	anywhere	Central, Town Hall, Wynyard, Circular Quay, St James & Museum, connecting to any train station	central Sydney hotels	Manly
Duration	to centre, 30min	to Central station, 15min	to central hotels, 30min	to Manly, 45min-1hr
Cost	to Central Station, $20-30; to Circular Quay, $30-40	to Central Station from domestic terminal single/return $14.50/22.20; from international terminal $14.80/22.60	single/return $13/22	single/return $37/70
Other		no service midnight-5am, otherwise every 15 min; return fares are cheaper after 9am & on weekends	no service 11pm-5am; bookings required	no service 11pm-5am; bookings required
Contact	see p176	Airport Link (☎ 13 15 00; www.airportlink.com.au)	Kingsford Smith Transport (☎ 9666 9988; www.kst.com.au)	Manly Airport Bus (☎ 0500 505 800; manlyairportbus @hotmail.com)

vegetable origin must be declared at customs. **Australian Customs** (☎ 1300 363 263; www.customs.gov.au) doesn't tolerate smugglers – don't even think about it. Travellers over 18 years can import 2.25L of liquor, 250 cigarettes or 250g of tobacco and dutiable goods up to the value of A$900 per person (A$450 for under 18s).

Australia has a 10% Goods and Services Tax (GST) automatically applied to most purchases, though some food items are exempt. If you purchase goods with a total minimum value of $300 from any one supplier within 30 days of departure from Australia, you're entitled to a GST refund. You can get a cheque refund at the designated booth located beyond Customs at Sydney Airport. Contact the **Australian Taxation Office** (☎ 13 28 66; www.ato.gov.au) for details.

GETTING AROUND

Central Sydney is very pedestrian-friendly; public transport is the best option for the surrounding suburbs. Trains, buses and ferries run by the **State Transit Authority of NSW** (STA; ☎ 13 15 00; www.131500.com.au) are convenient, reliable and good value. Contact STA for information or visit its Circular Quay information booths. Beware: the maximum fare-dodging fine is $550!

In this book, the nearest train/Monorail/Metro Light Rail/ferry station or bus route is noted after the 🚆 M 🚈 ⚓ or 🚌 icon in each listing.

RECOMMENDED MODES OF TRANSPORT

	Circular Quay	Bondi Beach	Kings Cross	Manly
Circular Quay	n/a	bus 40min	train 15min	Manly Fast Ferry 15min
Bondi Beach	bus 40min	n/a	bus to Bondi Junction 15min then train 15min	bus 40min then Manly Fast Ferry 15min
Kings Cross	train 15min	train to Bondi Junction 15min then bus 15min	n/a	train 15min then Manly Fast Ferry 15min
Manly	Manly Fast Ferry 15min	Manly Fast Ferry 15min then bus 40min	Manly Fast Ferry 15min then train 15min	n/a
Newtown	train 20min	train to Bondi Junction 30min then bus 15min	train 25min	train 20min then Manly Fast Ferry 15min
Paddington	bus 20min	bus 20min	bus 10min or walk 20min	bus 20 min then Manly Fast Ferry 15min
Surry Hills	bus 15min	bus 30min	bus 20min	bus 15min then Manly Fast Ferry 15min
Glebe	bus 20min	bus 20min then train to Bondi Junction then bus 15min	bus 20min then train 15min	bus 30min then Manly Fast Ferry 15min

TRAVEL PASSES

The good-value **SydneyPass** (☎ 13 15 00; www.sydneypass.info) includes bus, rail and ferry transport, travel on all the Sydney and Bondi Explorer buses (see p174), harbour ferry cruises (p61) and a return trip on the Airport Express train (p170). A three-/five-/ seven-day SydneyPass costs $115/150/170. It's available from the Sydney Visitor Centre (p180) at The Rocks and Darling Harbour, the Circular Quay Bus TransitShop and Sydney Ferries ticket offices, or onboard the Explorer buses.

The STA **DayTripper** (☎ 13 15 00; www.cityrail.info) is a day pass ($17) letting you ride on most trains, buses and ferries with discounts at an array of attractions. Available from STA ticket outlets.

BUS

Buses run almost everywhere, more slowly than trains. Bondi, Coogee and parts of the North

	Newtown	Paddington	Surry Hills	Glebe
	train 20min	bus 20min	bus 15min	bus 20min
	bus to Bondi Junction 15min then train 30min	bus 20min	bus 30min	bus 15min then train to Central then bus 20min
	train 25min	bus 10min or walk 20min	bus 20min	train 15min to Central then bus 20min
	Manly Fast Ferry 15min then train 20min	Manly Fast Ferry 15min then bus 20min	Manly Fast Ferry 15min then bus 15min	Manly Fast Ferry 15min then bus 30min
	n/a	bus 35min	bus 20min	bus 15min or walk 20min
	bus 35min	n/a	bus 10min, or walk 20min	bus 30min
	bus 20min	bus 10min or walk 20min	n/a	walk 10min then bus 20min
	bus 15min or walk 20min	bus 30min	bus 20min then walk 10min	n/a

Shore are serviced only by bus. Nightrider buses operate skeletally after regular buses and trains cease around midnight. Call the **Transport Infoline** (☎ 13 15 00; www.131500.com.au), or check the **Sydney Buses** (www.sydneybuses.info) website for details.

The main city bus stops are Circular Quay (Map p49, D3), Wynyard Park on York St (Map p33, A2) and Railway Square (Map pp66–7, D8). Many buses also stop outside the Queen Victoria Building on George and York Sts.

Buy tickets from newsagencies, Bus TransitShops and on buses (having the correct change will help). Fares start at $1.90; most trips are under $3.50. There are Bus TransitShops on the Alfred/Loftus St corner in Circular Quay (Map p49, D4), near Wynyard Station on Carrington St (Map p33, A2), and outside the Queen Victoria Building on York St (Map p33, A4), plus an information-only booth at Railway Square (Map p66–7, D8).

Bus routes starting with an X indicate limited-stop express routes; those with an L have limited stops. Bus routes listed in this book depart from Circular Quay unless otherwise indicated.

If you're taking public transport to Bondi or the Eastern Beaches, the quickest way is to take the train to Bondi Junction (between Woollahra and Bondi Beach), then jump on a bus.

Special Services

The STA's red **Sydney Explorer** (☎ 13 15 00; www.sydneypass.info/sydneyexplorer) bus follows a two-hour, 27-stop, hop-on, hop-off loop from Circular Quay through Kings Cross, Chinatown, Darling Harbour and

USEFUL BUS ROUTES FROM CIRCULAR QUAY

Place	Route No
Balmain	432-4, 441-2
Bondi Beach	380, 389 from Circular Quay, 381 from Bondi Junction
Coogee	372-4, 313-4 from Circular Quay, 353 from Bondi Junction
Darling Harbour	443, 456
Glebe	431-4
Kings Cross	323-7, 324-5, 333
Leichhardt	413, 435-8, 440
Manly	151, 169, E69 from Wynyard
Maroubra	376-7, 395-6, X77, X96
Newtown	422-3, 426, 428
Paddington	378, 380, 389
Surry Hills	301-4, 308-10, 343, 375, 390-1
Watsons Bay	324-5, L24 from Circular Quay, L82 from Bondi Junction

The Rocks, with pithy on-board commentary and discounted entry to attractions. Buses run every 20 minutes from 8.40am to 5.20pm; tickets cost adult/child $39/19 from drivers and Bus TransitShops.

Prices are identical for the blue **Bondi Explorer** (☎ 13 15 00; www.sydneypass.info/bondiexplorer) bus, which does a two-hour, 19-stop loop of the inner city and eastern suburbs, including Paddington, Double Bay, Vaucluse, Watsons Bay and Bondi Beach. Buses run every 30 minutes from 8.45am to 4.15pm.

CitySightseeing Sydney & Bondi Tours (☎ 9567 8400; www.city-sightseeing.com) is a privately run rival/alternative to the Explorer buses, with similar services and prices.

TRAIN

CityRail

Sydney's trains are the deft way to get around town. Trains run from around 5am to midnight. There are 24-hour ticket machines at most stations but humans are usually available too if you'd rather talk to something that'll listen. There's a **CityRail Information Booth** (Map p66-7, E7; ☎ 13 15 00; www.131500.com.au; ☽ 6am-10pm) at Central station near platforms four and five. For train routes, see the CityRail map on the pull-out sheet map.

Monorail

The **Metro Monorail** (☎ 9285 5600; www.metrotransport.com.au) is a lugubrious elevated worm circling around Darling Harbour and the city. A circuit costs $4.80; a day pass $9.50. The Monorail runs every four minutes from 7am to 10pm from Monday to Thursday, to midnight on Friday and Saturday, and from 8am to 10pm Sunday.

Metro Light Rail (MLR)

The future-slick **MLR** (☎ 9285 5600; www.metrotransport.com.au) glides between Central station and Pyrmont via Chinatown and Darling Harbour. A single ride costs between $3.20 and $5.70; a day pass $9. Trains run every 15 minutes from 6am to midnight, every 30 minutes from midnight to 6am. The service beyond Pyrmont to Lilyfield stops at 11pm Sunday to Thursday, midnight Friday and Saturday.

FERRY

Civilised **Sydney Ferries** (☎ 13 15 00; www.sydneyferries.info) runs regulation harbour ferries and RiverCats to Parramatta. There's also the new privately run **Manly Fast Ferry** (☎ 9583 1199; www.manlyfastferry.com.au). All services depart from Circular Quay. A one-way inner-harbour ferry ride costs around $5.20; the Manly Fast Ferry costs $8.20 one-way. Many ferries have connecting bus services.

TAXI

Taxis can be flagged down when their top-light is aglow. There are patrolled Friday/Saturday night taxi ranks around town, including one on Park St between Pitt and Castlereagh Sts, and at Central, Wynyard and Circular Quay stations. A short ride between the city and the inner suburbs will cost around $25; to/from the airport from $30 to $40. Some reliable operators:

Arrow Taxis (☎ 13 22 11)
Legion (☎ 13 14 51)
Premier Cabs (☎ 13 10 17)
Taxis Combined (☎ 8332 8888)

CAR & MOTORCYCLE

Masochistic? Bring your car into central Sydney. The city has a confusing spaghettilike one-way street system, parking is hell and parking inspectors are ruthless demons (also from hell). Tow-away zones prevail, and private car parks are expensive – around $15 per hour.

A car is, however, invaluable for exploring outer Sydney. Many hotels include parking in accommodation packages. Red-light and speed cameras are common. Sydney's motorways (including the Sydney Harbour Bridge and Tunnel) are electronically tolled; you'll need an RTA **E-Toll tag/pass** (☎ 13 18 65; www.rta.nsw.gov.au) or an **E-Way tag** (☎ 1300 555 833; www.tollpay .com.au) to use them.

PRACTICALITIES

BUSINESS HOURS

Banks, businesses and stores are closed on public holidays (opposite). Museums and other attractions often close on Christmas Day and Boxing Day. Banks open from 9.30am to 4pm Monday to Thursday, most until 5pm on Friday; some large city branches open from 8am to 6pm Monday to Friday. Post offices open 9am to 5pm Monday to Friday; some open 10am to 2pm on Saturday as well.

Businesses and shops open from 9am to 5pm Monday to Wednesday, Friday and Saturday, with late-night shopping until 9pm on Thursday. Sunday hours are usually 11am to 5pm. Pubs open from 11am to midnight; bars from around 4pm until late. Restaurants open around noon to 3pm for lunch, then close until dinner from 6pm to 10pm; some close on Sunday and/or Monday.

DISCOUNTS

Many attractions offer concession/ child/family/senior discounts. In this book concession prices are listed after adult prices (eg $15/7.50).

The **See Sydney & Beyond Card** (☎ 1300 661 711; www.seesydney card.com.au) offers admission to a wide range of Sydney's attractions including sightseeing tours, harbour cruises, museums, historic buildings and wildlife parks. One-/two-/three-/seven-day cards cost $75/135/165/225, available online or at the Sydney Visitor Centre (p180). The two-/three-/seven-day cards are also available with public transport included for $175/225/299.

The Heritage Housing Trust's (HHT) **Ticket Through Time** (☎ 8239 2288; www.hht.net.au) gets you into all 11 of the HHT's Sydney houses and museums, including Vaucluse House (p123), Government House (p50), Elizabeth Bay House (p97), Justice & Police Museum (p50), Museum of Sydney (p35), Hyde Park Barracks Museum (p35) and Susannah Place (p52). Tickets cost adult/concession/child/family $30/15/15/60; visit four or more sights and you'll save yourself a bit of hard-earned cash.

HOLIDAYS

New Year's Day 1 January
Australia Day 26 January
Good Friday & Easter Monday Late March/early April
Anzac Day 25 April
Queen's Birthday Second Monday in June
Bank Holiday First Monday in August
Labour Day First Monday in October
Christmas Day 25 December
Boxing Day 26 December

INTERNET

Internet cafés proliferate throughout Sydney, or you can jump online at public libraries and many hotels. Expect to pay anywhere between $2.50 and $5 per hour. Wireless access is increasingly popular.

Lonelyplanet.com offers speedy links to many of Sydney's websites. Other useful resources include the following:

Best Restaurants (www.bestrestaurants .com.au) Reviews, menus and booking info for the best eats on Sydney's streets.
Bureau of Meteorology (www.bom.gov.au) Should I bring a jacket, or will a T-shirt be OK?
Sydney City Council (www.cityofsydney.nsw .gov.au) All the boring stuff, plus festival and events listings.
Sydney City Guide (www.citysearch.com .au) Harbour town news, arts, eating and entertainment news.
Surf Report (www.realsurf.com) Check the swell and get among it.

LANGUAGE

If you're not from Australia, you'll find the local lingo (Strine) to be colourful, disarming and bamboozling all at once. Lonely Planet's *Australian Language & Culture* is the definitive pocket-sized guide, but here's a handful of Strine essentials:
arvo afternoon
barbie barbecue
beaut, **bewdy**, **bonza** superb
bloke man
bludger lazy oaf
bugger off depart with haste (earnest instruction)

crack the shits to express utmost irritation
crook ill or substandard
dead horse tomato sauce, ketchup
dead set yes, that's correct
dunny toilet
fair dinkum honest, genuine
flaming galah foolish individual
flat out really busy or fast
footy football (Australian Rules or Rugby League)
g'day hello
hard yakka hard work
mate generic informal address
mozzie mosquito
no worries, no wukkin furries everything's under control
piss beer
see ya goodbye
sheila woman
shoot through leave
strewth annoyed exclamation
taking the piss humorous deception
tinnie aluminium boat or beer can
true blue authentically Australian
tucker food
youse more than one person

MEDICAL SERVICES
Hospitals with 24-hour accident and emergency departments include the following:
Royal Prince Alfred Hospital (Map p77, C4; ☎ 9515 6111; www.cs.nsw.gov.au/rpa; Missenden Rd, Camperdown)
St Vincent's Hospital (Map pp98-9, D7; ☎ 8382 7111; wwwsvh.stvincents.com.au; cnr Victoria & Burton Sts, Darlinghurst)
Sydney Hospital & Sydney Eye Hospital (Map p33, C3; ☎ 9382 7111; www.sesahs.nsw.gov.au/sydhosp; 8 Macquarie St)

MONEY
CURRENCY
The Australian dollar is divided into 100 cents. When paying with cash, prices are rounded up or down to the nearest 5 cents. There are coins for $2, $1, 50¢, 20¢, 10¢ and 5¢; notes for $100 (an 'avocado'), $50 (a 'pineapple'), $20 (a 'lobster'), $10 and $5.

COSTS
Not including accommodation, an average Sydney day with midrange restaurant meals, public transport, sight admission, a taxi ride and a couple of beers at the pub will set you back $150 to $200.

American Express, Diners Club, MasterCard and Visa credit cards are all widely accepted. Travellers cheques are accepted in banks, large hotels and duty-free stores; those in Australian dollars can generally be exchanged at banks without fees. There are 24-hour ATMs at most banks, and some pubs and clubs. Shops and retail outlets have Eftpos facilities for on-the-spot debit-card payments.

NEWSPAPERS & MAGAZINES
Daily newspapers include the tabloid *Daily Telegraph* (www.dailytelegraph.news.com.au) and the broadsheets *Sydney Morning*

Herald (www.smh.com.au), the *Australian* (www.theaustralian.news.com.au) and the *Australian Financial Review* (www.afr.com).

Magazines worth looking at include the foodie mag *Delicious* (www.deliciousmagazine.com.au), *Time* (www.time.com), and Australia's versions of *Rolling Stone* (www.rollingstone.com). For fashion and design, check out *GQ* (www.vogue.com.au/in_vogue/gq) and *Vogue Australia* (www.vogue.com.au).

Free street press covering local music and entertainment shenanigans includes alt-rock mags *Drum Media* (www.drummedia.com.au) and the *Brag* (www.myspace.com/thebrag), and *3D World* (clubbing and dance; www.threedworld.com.au). *This Week in Sydney* is a free tourist mag. Also check out the free nightly tabloid *MX* (www.mxnet.com.au) and the gay and lesbian *SX* (www.evolutionpublishing.com.au).

POST

Stamps are sold at post offices in most suburbs and most newsagencies. It costs 55¢ to send a postcard or standard letter within Australia. Airmail letters (weighing up to 50g) cost $1.40 to the Asia/Pacific region; $2.05 to the rest of the world. Postcards to anywhere outside Australia cost $1.35.

TELEPHONE

Public payphones are either coin- or card-operated; local calls cost 50¢. Many also accept credit cards. Local and international phonecards range in value from $5 to $50 – look for the phonecard logo on display at retail outlets.

Mobile phone numbers have four-digit prefixes beginning with 04. Australia's digital network is compatible with GSM 900 and 1800 handsets (used in Europe). Quad-band US phones will work, but to avoid global-roaming charges you'll need an unlocked handset that takes prepaid SIM cards from Australian providers such as **Telstra** (www.telstra.com), **Optus** (www.optus.com.au), **Virgin** (www.virginmobile.com.au) or **Vodafone** (www.vodafone.com.au).

TIPPING

Like the rest of Australia, tipping in Sydney isn't mandatory, but it's polite to tip hotel porters $2 per bag, and taxis and restaurant waiters around 10% of the charge.

TOURIST INFORMATION

There are **City Host Information Kiosks** at Circular Quay (Map p49, D4) and on George St outside the Town Hall (Map p33, A5), while **Tourism Australia** (www.australia.com) conducts customer relations through its website. Also worth a try:

National Parks & Wildlife Service (NPWS; Map p49, D3; ☎ 9247 5033; www .environment.nsw.gov.au; Cadman's Cottage, 110 George St, The Rocks; 🕑 9.30am-4.30pm Mon-Fri, 10am-4.30pm Sat & Sun; 🚇 🚌 ⚓ Circular Quay) Info on Sydney Harbour, Royal, Ku-ring-gai Chase and Blue Mountains national parks.

National Roads & Motorists Association (NRMA; Map p33, A3; ☎ 13 21 32, emergency assistance 13 11 11; 74-76 King St; 🕑 9am-5pm Mon-Fri; 🚇 Martin Place Ⓜ City Centre 🚌 George St buses) Provides 24-hour emergency roadside assistance, and travel insurance and accommodation advice.

Sydney Visitor Centre (www.sydneyvisit orcentre.com) Circular Quay (Map p49, C3; ☎ 9240 8788; cnr Argyle & Playfair Sts, The Rocks; 🕑 9.30am-5.30pm; 🚇 🚌 ⚓ Circular Quay) Darling Harbour (Map pp66-7, C4; ☎ 9240 8788; 🕑 9.30am-5.30pm; 🚇 Town Hall Ⓜ Garden Plaza 🚌 Convention ⚓ Darling Harbour) Super comprehensive, also acting as an accommodation agency (last minute and in advance).

Tourism NSW (☎ 9931 1111; www.visitnsw .com) Statewide accommodation and travel advice.

Tourist Information Service (☎ 9669 5111; 🕑 7am-10pm) Sydney-centric information and accommodation phone service.

Travellers' Information Service (Map pp66-7, E7; ☎ 9281 9366; Sydney Coach Terminal, Eddy Ave; 🕑 6am-6pm Mon-Fri, 8am-6pm Sat & Sun; 🚇 Central Ⓜ Haymarket 🚌 George St buses) Helpful, busy office handling last-minute accommodation bookings, coach tickets, public transport information and maps.

TRAVELLERS WITH DISABILITIES

Most of Sydney's attractions are accessible to travellers with wheelchairs. All new or renovated venues cater for wheelchairs but older buildings are harder to access. Most of the National Trust's historic houses are at least partially accessible – abashed attendants can usually show you photos of inaccessible areas.

Taxis can usually accommodate wheelchairs; Sydney has a proliferation of parking spaces reserved for disabled drivers. Most of Sydney's major attractions offer hearing loops and sign language interpreters for hearing-impaired travellers. Check in advance.

For more info contact the following organisations:

City of Sydney (☎ 9265 9333; www.city ofsydney.nsw.gov.au) Lists venues with good wheelchair access.

Deaf Society of NSW (☎ 9893 8555; www .deafsocietynsw.org.au) Services, events and resources around Sydney.

Roads & Traffic Authority (☎ 13 22 13; www.rta.nsw.gov.au) For disabled parking permits.

Spinal Cord Injuries Australia (☎ 9661 8855; www.spinalcordinjuries.com.au) Publishes *Access Sydney*.

Vision Australia (☎ 1300 847 466; www .visionaustralia.org.au) Services, events and resources.

>INDEX

See also separate subindexes for See (p188), Shop (p189), Eat (p190), Drink (p191) and Play (p191).

000 map pages

SEE

Churches
St James' Church 36

Galleries
Aboriginal Fine Art Prints 97
Art Gallery of NSW 18, 34
Artery 97
Artspace 97
Australian Centre for
    Photography 112
Australian Galleries 112
Brett Whiteley Studio 90
Ceramic Art Gallery 112
Gannon House 50
Hogarth Galleries 112
Iain Dawson Gallery 112
Manly Art Gallery &
    Museum 134
Object Gallery 90
Original & Authentic
    Aboriginal Art 51
Ray Hughes Gallery 91
SH Ervin Gallery 51-2
Wagner Art Gallery 113
Watters Gallery 37

Museums
Australian Museum 35
Australian National Maritime
    Museum 65
Hyde Park Barracks Museum
    35
Justice & Police Museum 50

INDEX

000 map pages